Seedlings From The Smoke

Musings of an Urban Market Gardener

OrganicLea Community Growers

ORGANICLEA

First published 2014 by
OrganicLea Community Growers
Hawkwood Community Plant Nursery
115 Hawkwood Crescent
London E4 7UH

Text by Ru Litherland, originally published online
at www.organiclea.wordpress.com
Illustrations by Marlene Barrett
Photographs by OrganicLea and friends
Back cover *Barcode Runaway* image with thanks to Adbusters.org
Edit and design by Louisa Wright,
Dave McTaggart, Hannah Leigh Mackie, Clare Joy
Printed by Calverts Co-operative on 100% recycled paper
using vegetable-oil based inks. www.calverts.coop

ISBN 978-0-9931025-0-9

OrganicLea Ltd
Registered office address:
Hornbeam Centre
458 Hoe Street
Walthamstow
London
E17 9AH

www.organiclea.org.uk

**The Entrance Field at Hawkwood Community Plant Nursery,
September 2014**
Weeding amongst the "Jack Be Little" pumpkins

Contents

2 Foreword by David Ransom

6 Introduction

14 January

24 February

42 March

60 April

76 May

96 June

114 July

132 August

146 September

168 October

184 November

196 December

208 Endnotes

For those who shed sweat onto gardens and farms,
onto grocers' grass, cookers, who are up to their arms
in it; who sweep onto the streets
and public places; who vote with their feet;
who put their money where their mouth is;
who are what they eat;

For you,
Nothing is wasted, everything for keeps.

Welcome to Hawkwood Community Plant Nursery (2012)
Your journey starts here, at the Propagation Station

Foreword

I first came across OrganicLea in the spring of 2007. The project was, I had heard, already a strong thread in a network growing rapidly across London and, indeed, around the wider world. It was being woven into a form of tribute to nature, turning neglected nooks and crannies to creative use, producing and distributing fresh food near to the places where most of us now eat, in towns and cities.

The valley of the River Lea, cutting through London's East End, has generally been taken by the people who live nearby — as I did for many years — as wasteland: rarely visited, vaguely forbidding, hazardous, perforated by the city's plumbing, pylons, railway tracks, polluted industrial sites, the occasional cult pub, bird sanctuary, marina or oasis for wholesome physical pursuits. The corseted river itself, legend has it, is at this point so infused with the urine of rats that to fall into it is to have an untimely meeting with one's maker.

The mouth of the valley, at the River Thames, had just been concealed behind miles of blue hoarding and subjected to a brutal "regeneration" for the lavish corporate jamboree of the 2012 London Olympics. Further upstream the river flows beneath the orbital M25, taken to mark the outer boundary of the metropolis.

So, roughly midway between the two in Waltham Forest — once a stamping ground for William Morris — I arrived at OrganicLea half expecting to find the equivalent of a sapling in the central reservation of a motorway. I discovered, if not the Garden of Eden itself, then that rare, distinctive scent of growth, at once fertile and powerful, between the good nature of people — Ru Litherland among them — the vast, bewildering colonies we have formed and the one earth we all have to inhabit.

I was promptly deployed to cover footpaths with disused fairtrade coffee sacks from Guatemala and Peru. Beads of sweat smudged my notes. Failing limbs snatched the odd, truly lamentable snapshot. My mask of objective observation slipped. Or maybe it was just that some of those really cool people turned out to live, as I do, on boats. Whatever. Recovering afterwards, that much fitter, the brilliance of the project struck me as unbearably brittle. My guts were gripped by foreboding, as they regularly are by anything at all promising.

I need not have feared. As Ru Litherland suggests in his wonderful book: "Bad things sometimes happen. The good news is, they often don't."

So now, seven years on, we have Hawkwood — and this immensely enjoyable, informative, inspiring, beguiling, self-effacing, funny, invaluable account of its infancy. The "urban market garden" has evidently been transplanted, grown and flourished, well beyond my fondest hopes. Besides, as the author bids us: "To say, as I've heard it said, 'it ends badly' is like drawing a full stop on the seasons: there is no ending, happy or bad: we have to keep going."

Hot Stuff (2013)

Hawkwood's "World of Chillies" collection features varieties from all corners of the globe

Thus far, at my lengthening age, I have. All the same, and naturally enough, without food I would have come to a halt some time ago. Yet the production of food currently consumes a third of all the strictly limited amount of carbon fossils with which, in multiple ways, we are still poisoning ourselves. A third of the food made for the people of "developed" societies goes to waste. While a third of humanity staggers towards obesity, another third can't be sure where to find its next meal. Some people have even taken to arguing that we were all much better off in the Stone Age. And to this there is said to be no alternative.

In such mean times, high expectations – mine included – can strangle brilliant projects like Hawkwood. If they have not saved the world already, they have failed. If they threaten to save the world anytime soon, they are dangerous. If they do not aim to save the world at all, they are irrelevant. If they do not make money, they will die. If they do make money, they can't save the world. So you see, there really is no alternative!

"People don't want lives of drudgery and poverty," Ru Litherland observes, "but working the land no more has to be that than does being a professional athlete, a computer programmer, or a postie: it's just how our weird world has ordered it. So it can be re-ordered, little by little, step by step, bottom to top."

Keeping one's ear to the ground and peripheral vision in focus at the same time is a tricky skill. Ru Litherland has made an art of it, with a breadth and depth of perception that sometimes speaks through fable and poetry, bringing to my mind at least the great Uruguayan writer Eduardo Galeano.

Freed from hindsight, you can follow the troublesome stories of heritage vegetables, of Walthamstow Yellow Cress, Kondine Red or Essex Wonder tomatoes, and the author's temperamental affection for them – only chilli peppers seem to have kept him entirely loyal – as they happen, as if they were alive. You can glimpse, too, the Zapatistas in Chiapas, slow food in Tuscany, champagne rhubarb in the Yorkshire Triangle. Another real world already exists.

And, all the while, as if by sleight of hand, you find you are being shown something worth seeing with fresh eyes – the perverse exuberance of nature, the "bland capitalist monoculture creating a global weather system after its own image". You may even have been given a clearer idea of what to do next.

In April 2012 "winter came hard and late, like Paul Scholes on one of his bad days." Whatever the likeness between the play of a Manchester United footballer and April – the "cruellest month" in TS Eliot's "The Wasteland" – you know you are being treated to a gardener's diary like no other.

Or, as Ru Litherland has it: "Every start starts with an end, or is it every end ends with a start? I always get muddled. Anyway, the point being that, in the endless breathtaking rally between seasonal superfoods, strawberries bounce up exactly where rhubarb and asparagus leave off."

Quite so.

Enjoy!

David Ransom
A co-editor of *New Internationalist* magazine between 1989 and 2009

Introduction

The year is 2000, a new millennium, and the battery chickens are coming home to roost. Britain, birthplace of industrial agriculture, is experiencing wave after wave of food crises: salmonella, mad cow disease, dietary illnesses such as heart disease and obesity, pesticide poisoning. The spectres of genetic modification, total supermarket control, climate change associated with "food miles" and farming, loom dangerously close.

Unnoticed by Tesco executives, three women are riding bicycles up the River Lea towpath from East London to Hertfordshire, when they encounter some derelict glasshouses. In one pannier is a copy of *The Book of the River Lea* by Margaret Ashby, containing a chapter on the Lea Valley's once vast sea of market gardens.

HERE seemed a good place to start growing a new food system, one that cares for people and planet. Or as we later put it less snappily, to sustainably rehabilitate the food-growing heritage of the Lea Valley. OrganicLea was born.

There were the early drinkings in meeting venues in central London – the Blue Posts on Newman Street, the Africa Centre, gathering together a small cell of people prepared to take the idea forward. There was the proposal, sent out to over one hundred public institutions and civil society organisations across the "Lea Valley bioregion", a geologically defined land area that spreadeagles across the latter day council borders of Tower Hamlets, Newham, Hackney, Haringey, Waltham Forest, Enfield, Broxbourne, Epping Forest and East Herts. There was the widespread disinterest, and only the London Borough of Waltham Forest offering practical support in the form of derelict allotments. There were the fundraising evenings at Bonnington Café in Vauxhall for basic tools. Then, on 10 February 2001, there came the official launch: not of a flag up a pole, but of a fork in the soil, as a handful of people got to grips with the bramble patch that was to become, for the next rich seven years, the beating heart of OrganicLea's campaign for community food.

Much of the work at Drysdale allotments was carried out on two work days per month, when whoever showed up to help out could take home their share of the day's harvest. This still left plenty of produce for a mini box scheme in 2001, and occasional produce stalls at local events, where the fresh and sometimes hilariously shaped veg helped to draw people in and draw ideas and connections out. It probably drove a few folk away too, but you can't please all the people all the time.

As the growing site stabilised, energy could spiral outwards into what we would later term our training and outreach activities: in 2001 to 2003 we ran more café nights, this time at the Hornbeam Centre in Walthamstow, in which food, culture and politics were stirred together, with results that were messy and inspired.

In 2003/04 we ran our first organic gardening training courses at the allotment site, and partnered with Leyton Surestart to organise a low-price produce stall for parents at Beaumont Community centre. In 2005, Brian started making a nuisance of himself, knocking on doors of houses in whose back gardens he spotted ripe fruit.

Golden Delicious (2013)
The young orchard cradled by mature oaks

Too many people humoured him by letting him gather the soon-to-be-windfalls, that we were only encouraged to unleash the "Scrumping Project" the following year, one of our most popular and continuing ventures, where unwanted fruit from domestic gardens and public areas is rescued and poured back into the local food system.

In summer 2006, we organised a meeting on community food at Vestry House, Walthamstow. Five years on from our original, widely (and probably justifiably) ignored proposal, fifty participants representing a host of local community and health groups came together to discuss ways in which Waltham Forest residents could get better food. Out of this came the idea of the "Food Hub", a weekly stall selling the whole range of local, organic fruit and veg at the Hornbeam Centre, around which other food events, workshops and information sharing could be organised.

We worked with Eostre Organics, a cooperative of growers in East Anglia, to establish the stall on the corner of Bakers Avenue, in September 2006, to a rousing chorus of enthusiasm, scepticism and ambivalence. And there it's traded ever since, in all weathers, good times and bad. I suppose it's what you'd now call a fixture. At the same time, we commissioned research into the legal situation regarding sales of allotment produce, resulting in the briefing paper: "Selling Allotment Produce: Is it Legal? Is It Right?" [i]. On the back of this we launched the "Cropshare" scheme, enabling home and allotment gardeners to share or trade their surplus fruit and veg through the stalls. The Lottery's *Making Local Food Work* programme funded the development of the "Local Food Centre" as the "Food Hub" became known.

This included ongoing support for the Hornbeam Café, which in turn makes a mission of mopping up any unsold produce; and also the launch of another outlet for local produce, our weekly box scheme, in 2008.

At the outset of OrganicLea, as with any new project, it was all excitement, vision and paradigm-shifting possibilities. As the years rolled on, we never seemed to arrive at the post-norming stage; we hadn't become a professional, middle-of-the-road outfit that ticked its boxes and shed its more leftfield ideas. The food scandals didn't let up, and more and more people were seeing local, organic food as one important way to address the environmental crisis, and perhaps the related economic and social crises. We got invited places; we pushed doors and they opened. A list of community food projects and events bore our sticky fingerprints. One was the "Linear Orchard", a partnership with the council whereby a cycle path connecting Walthamstow and Chingford was to be planted with fruit trees. The council provided the trees, while, in an effort to encourage awareness and a sense of ownership, we worked with local community groups – in this case the school, allotment association and traveller site – to plant the trees.

Visiting Hawkwood Central Nursery, just five minutes away from Drysdale allotments, to collect said trees in February 2007, we were met by the impressive site of the glasshouses and growing area, and by disgruntled workers, who told us this was their last job: the place was closing down next month. We rushed off a proposal to the council for the premises to be put over to a "community plant nursery and market garden", and heard no more. As is more poetically recounted in Robin Grey's song "The Ballad of Hawkwood" [ii], the council came back to us over a year later, in the absence of a better offer or permission for a change of land use, offering us a lease on the nursery, its buildings, its twelve acres of land, half an acre of it under one million pounds worth of glass structure.

Be careful what you wish for, they say. The council offer coincided with our lowest point in terms of members: four people in August 2008, all busy doing plenty of other things thank you very much. But it was an offer we couldn't refuse, even without horses' heads and threats of violence that often accompany such things. Seven years in though, as Blind Mole Rat sang of the Zapatistas, "we ain't got no bosses, we just got a lot of friends" [iii]. We had, by that stage, met and worked with many folk, somewhere close to where community development meets gardening. The Hawkwood Steering Group of fourteen was formed.

Informed by permaculture, the first year of our tenure was light on the growing, as we sought to survey and analyse – the land, our organisation and the wider community – in order to arrive at a design that would work, while being true to the permaculture ethics of "earth care, people care, fair shares". The result was "Hawkwood Community Plant Nursery – for Plants and People" [iv]: a booklet capturing the design findings, a business plan, and with that, three years' start-up funding from the National Lottery Food Fund, for which we are eternally grateful.

During the course of the organisational design, the Hawkwood Steering Group elected that the Hawkwood project become part of OrganicLea workers' cooperative; and soon afterwards Common Sense Growers, a local group specialising in food growing outreach and support in all kinds of public spaces – from schools to housing estates to women's refuges – also applied to join us.

Thus, in October 2009, a new chapter for OrganicLea: a ten-person cooperative, now composed largely of contracted, waged workers; a scaling up of production, and training and volunteering work, with a 12-acre site, buildings and soon-to-be classroom; and a whole other string to our bow, with barefoot gardeners taking it out to the streets and grassroots, under our auspices. This began to look like a coherent programme of small-scale social transformation. So much so we were able to define our mission and vision as being:

OrganicLea is a community food project based in the Lea Valley in north-east London. We produce and distribute food and plants locally, and inspire and support others to do the same. With a workers' cooperative at our core, we bring people together to take action towards a more just and sustainable society.

Our vision is of a socially and environmentally just food system where the means of production and distribution, including access to land, seed and water are controlled not by markets or corporations but by the people themselves. We are working to create just production and trading systems that provide a fair income to food producers and guarantee the rights of communities to access healthy and nutritious food produced using ecologically sound and sustainable methods, a food system existing in a wider context of social justice.

There was a final piece in the jigsaw: while we had pushed for wider change in line with our local aims and vision in an ad hoc way since the offing, the arrival of Adam as "System Change Worker" in 2012 ensures that educating, campaigning and organising on issues of food, farming and environment is now part of our core work.

What comes next is the story of OrganicLea – the Hawkwood Years. This story will be told in an idiosyncratic fashion in the ensuing pages, but here are the headline grabbers:

Since its opening as a community plant nursery and market garden in October 2009, Hawkwood has:

- Hosted over 800 volunteers and over 3,000 visitors
- Installed a straw-bale classroom: 780 adult learners have completed courses here in gardening and land-based subjects such as natural beekeeping and permaculture, unaccredited and accredited, up to Level 2
- Land: two acres under intensive vegetable production, two acres of fruit production, and the rest managed for biodiversity
- Harvested and distributed over 30,000 kilos of fresh produce
- Run eighty plant stalls at Hawkwood and community events. Our plants have helped to stock dozens of community gardens across London. Overall, we've raised over 150,000 plants at the Nursery.

As well as this:

- Our Open Days attract between 20 and 60 people every month, for site tours and attractions ranging from herbal walks to chilli lectures to community wine making. We were proud to host "Transforming Our Food System" in 2012, a conference attended by 110 food campaigners, which helped to launch the Food Sovereignty movement in the UK.
- In October 2012, the box scheme moved to Hawkwood. Over these two years we have seen our box scheme numbers double; we now distribute 280 bags per week to 12 community pick up points across the borough.
- In 2010 we opened a second weekly produce stall on Leytonstone High Road, in partnership with Transition Leytonstone. We now have up to 100 regular customers per week.
- Our produce is currently on the menu in 16 local restaurants and available in two local grocers, from our local community café The Hornbeam, to high-end restaurants such as the Clove Club and Opera Tavern.
- In 2014/15 we will be spending £120,000 on local produce, supporting local organic farmers in East Anglia and Kent, Hawkwood Plant Nursery and a myriad of local "Cropshare" and "Grubshare" suppliers.
- 2014/15 will see our enterprise and distribution work turnover hitting £170,000. Reports published this year by the Local Food Fund have demonstrated this brings with it a six- to eight-fold increase in social and economic value to our local community. That's a million-pound value milestone!
- We have been directly involved in the growth of over fifty food gardens with community partners, including schools, housing associations, community centres and supported housing gardens, in Waltham Forest and neighbouring boroughs.
- We have played an active role in the formation and development of the Community Food Growers' Network in London, and the national Landworkers' Alliance.

Taking a broader view, the ideas and concerns that catalysed the formation of OrganicLea in 2001 were at the time fringe, and have, in the thirteen years hence, become more widely accepted. Too often the little people, like OrganicLea and similar initiatives, are regarded as beneficiaries of the zeitgeist. But let's remember we are also its creators, by working creatively to change opinions and culture from the bottom up. Community food projects have mushroomed, so that every town has at least one, if not a dozen, and awareness of and demand for local, seasonal, organic produce is at an all-time high. Food growing is back on the national school curriculum. Everyone in the food business now is trying to present what they do as in tune with the demand for something more direct, more local, more natural. Some of this is authentic; some is clever marketing; some is out-and-out lies. In advanced capitalism, you can win the *struggle for hegemony*[v] – the battle for ideas – and then the struggle continues: you have to go back and show how these ideas have been coopted and betrayed, because, as John Lennon elegantly put it, "the same bastards are in control".

And this is what it's about too – about people taking back control of their communities, their spaces, their basic human needs, their lives – as a necessary precursor to any "system change"; and also to create the "new world in the shell of the old": to build the kind of systems, structures and ways of working that we can safely, graciously fall back on, if and when the corrupt old order really starts to crumble.[vi]

From the outset, then, it's never been about growing food in and of itself, but about its potential role in feeding real regeneration by restoring social and environmental health. Once we had begun working at Hawkwood in earnest, Clare, the Promotions and Distribution Worker, suggested that, in addition to the various methods of promoting our ideas and activities already in use, we add a "Grower's Blog", providing a wider audience with a current account of what is going on in the community market garden.

This seemed a perfectly common sense suggestion and, as the newly appointed Plants & Production Worker, I agreed to posting this on a regular to occasional basis. Marlene, the Finance & Communications Worker, designed the page, and we settled on the strapline of "musings of an urban market gardener". This turned out to be a disturbingly accurate summary of the contents, which I'm not sure were quite what Clare had in mind as a web-based showcase of our work. But I was having so much fun with it I clean forgot to check in with her for the first few months, by which time it was already too late: the blogs had developed a peculiar life of their own, becoming, as hoped, a chronicle of the times of Hawkwood Community Plant Nursery, albeit a somewhat meandering one.

Whatever their shortcomings as an historical account, they have achieved one other thing they set out to do at the start. That is, to use modern media to carry a form that is truly ancient: the gardener's diary. And, like all gardeners' diaries public and private, they store up the snatchings of successes, failures, feelings and smells that arise from the soil, via the plants, as observed by the otherwise myopic, harassed gardener.

Then, as we reached the end of a four-year rotation since the seed of the blog idea was sown, there began to grow a notion that it might be about time to harvest some ripe tales from the cyberspace, to preserve and present them in the tangible, romantic form of a book.

The passages are presented on a month-by-month basis, taking us through the Gardening Year, and the calendar five years. We have resisted the temptation to edit them in hindsight, presenting them, mildew and all, as they were originally entered, except for the odd typo. We have however, dropped a few entries and added endnotes, to remind the reader of "news" events that are referred to, passingly, in the text.

The original blog posts also wove in direct quotes and sideways references to songs, people and movements; and, seeing as endnotes are now there, we've used them to make these references more explicit, for those that would like them to be.

While any views, blues and loose screws expressed in the chapters are, classically, not necessarily those of OrganicLea workers' cooperative, the wider OrganicLea family or indeed our resident insects; and while they are penned – usually pencilled actually – then laboriously typed up by my hand; everything that inspires and provokes them is the product of collective effort and intelligence, and thus the credit and, I'm glad to say, blame for the authorship rests firmly with the collective. I return often to the passage from Keri Hulme's *The Bone People*, that Clare and Anthony Assis selected for the 2011 photographic exhibition of food growing in Waltham Forest:

"They were nothing more than people, by themselves. Even paired, any pairing, they would have been nothing more than people by themselves. But all together, they have become the heart and muscles and mind of something perilous and new, something strange and growing and great.

Together, all together, they are the instruments of change." [vii]

Ru Litherland
August 02014 [viii]

i.   www.organiclea.org.uk/publications.

ii. From the album The Nearest Door (2010).
     http://music.robingrey.com/track/the-ballad-of-hawkwood.

iii. Blind Mole Rat, Viva Zapata!, Round Records, 1994.

iv. Hawkwood Nursery, for Plants and People: a journey in permaculture design (2009).
     See www.organiclea.org.uk/publications.

v.   The "struggle for hegemony" was a concept originally developed by Antonio Gramsci. He defined hegemony as "moral and political leadership, which manages to win the active consent of those over whom it rules". In doing so, he alerted social movements to the notion that culture and ideas were a necessary "arena for struggle" as well as political and economic institutions. Antonio Gramsci, Further Selections from the Prison Notebooks. University of Minnesota, 1995.

vi. For a more detailed discussion on the politics of community food projects, see R. Litherland's 2010 essay, "Where Next For The Community Food Movement?".

vii. Keri Hulme, The Bone People. Spiral Press, 1984.

viii. 02012: occasionally in the text the calendar year is a five-digit number beginning with "0". This is a device of the "Long Now" movement, an attempt to encourage long-term thinking and planning on this planet. See www.longnow.org.

HAWKWOOD NURSERY

FOR PLANTS AND PEOPLE

Yates' Meadow ↑

APIARY

ORCHARD

VINEYARD

OLD KITCHEN GARDEN

OAK GROVE

KEN'S MAGICAL REALM

WEST BANK TERRACES

RASPBERRY ROW

FRED & CAROL'S

COMPOST

CHERRY BANK

SPRING FIELD

WELL

Epping Forest

GLASSHOUSE

ENTRANCE FIELD

POETS CORNER

London ↙

January

Snow Patrol (2013)
Hawkwood's transport & logistics division is rarely troubled by winter weather

London Underground

January 25, 2010

The early peas in the glasshouse, which were laid low by the penetrative frosts a mere week ago, are showing signs of recovery: many are clinging for dear life to their mesh support, their threadlike tendrils winching them up towards the glimmer of light. Often plants have a way of expressing what's going on as well as any human.

In the adjacent "East Wing", the shoots of garlic (garlic and peas aren't considered good neighbours in companion planting orthodoxy — the glass doors are shut and I don't think they've seen each other yet) are altogether more assertive in their thrusting out of the ground. You have to admire their confidence, but their progress is tortuously slow.

Clare's been striking our first hardwood cuttings (blackcurrant and worcesterberry). Striking is a magnificent verb to perform, and people don't get to do it enough nowadays. They're going into pots for now whilst we are digging a nursery and cuttings bed to the west of the glasshouse. This has meant painstakingly re-homing hundreds of the lawn's current daffodil bulb inhabitants, their shoots looking identical to those of their garlic cousins. Every piece of ground, however unpromising, has within it life, history and spring.

Diggers All

January 31, 2010

"It was no thought or word that called culture into being, but a tool or a weapon. After the stone axe we needed song and story to remember innocence, to record effect — and so to describe the limits, to say what can be done without damage.

The use only of our bodies for work or love or pleasure, or even for combat, sets us free again in the wilderness, and we exalt...But a man with a machine and inadequate culture...is a pestilence. He shakes more than he can hold". -Wendell Berry, Damage[1]

This year, my growing activity has "scaled up", from half an acre to the 12 acres at Hawkwood. How to work that much more space? Well, for one thing, most of the production will be more "extensive" – perennial fruit and vegetables, and field veg – alongside the high maintenance salad leaves and glasshouse crops. Then there's People Power, big happy gangs turning up for hard rewarding tasks like fencing, tree planting, raised bed building. We are welcoming in new hand tools, those used in broader-scale horticulture, such as scythes, wheel hoes and seeders. And then there's powered machines.

We've bought a Goldoni Jolly walking tractor, as used by small farmers and peasants over Europe and beyond. I like its relative lightness and the fact that when using it you still have your feet firmly on the ground.

Roger has managed to get the abandoned and condemned old council tractor up and running. It's a beast of a machine and is unsurpassed when it comes to transporting large bulky loads, such as woodchip and compost, around the place. Huf, the "Buildings and facilities" coordinator, has among his rare claims the fact that he has built a biodiesel plant, so we have the potential to run vehicles off "waste" veg oil. To this end we have been patronising the local chippy, in a bid to ingratiate ourselves with future suppliers, with considerable vigour over these cold barren months.

Last week we hired a mini-digger to accomplish some of the larger earthworks. In permaculture, "mechanical solutions" like this are regarded as acceptable one-offs in setting up structures and systems which then enable more effective biological processes to continue. It made light work of digging a swale across the Entrance Field, but created a huge mess on the West Terrace, churning and compacting the sodden clay until finally, the digger itself acknowledged the hopelessness of the exercise, slumping resolutely into the mud bath.

I had visions of having to hire a bigger digger to try to fish it out, leading us into a farce that might climax with the world's biggest digger crunching over the glasshouse to the rescue. In the event, it only took four people, one tractor, 20 jute sacks, 8 scaffold boards, 14 swear words and 2 hours for digger and hard standing to be reunited. We are just beginning to learn the limits of machines, of the land, of each others' patience.

Back to the Garden

January 22, 2012

Today, my shadow touched the garden after four weeks' absence. That's a long time in human affairs, but in January, barely worth two summer days of plant growth. That's a pretty good exchange rate: I've been spending some time abroad.

After the festive season, this year's winter break was spent in warmer climes. The official line is that this allows me to be outside amongst plants that are active, though sceptics might wryly note the "topped up" status of my suntan.

Andalucia, in Southern Spain, has a rich, living horticultural tradition. We stayed at Chris and Terry's Finca Colina in Barranca. Not far inland from the dense golden honeypot of the Costa del Sol, it's a tranquil tapestry of smallholdings, shielded from unbalanced development by its sheer topography. Each lime-washed house balances among its steep few acres of extensive olive and almonds. Extensive, as the relative financial return on such land is too low now for most, except the goat herders, to work it full time.

This presumably assists the wild plants of the understory, so that on my kernel-warming wanderings under almond blossom I would meet more salad burnet, mountain thyme, apple mint, fennel and navelwort than I could hope to use.

One of the magics of real travel, or just stopping still to see things differently, is the surprise of the familiar, like the common-or-garden plants listed above — interlaced with the bafflingly exotic. Out of this foreign language of flowers emerged some moments of enlightenment: an endemic thorny specimen was pointed out as wild asparagus, the shoots of which we later found in abundance at Algeciras market. The larger of the many cork-skinned evergreens in this dry land identified itself as a carob: by their fruits shall thee know them.

On the track homewards, the many railside cultivations looked like allotments, only different. The town of Ronda was a leader, but not unique, in lining its streets with orange trees. From bitter experience, I can confirm these to be marmalade, rather than dessert, types. In Madrid, Emilio, a founder member of OrganicLea, tried to dispel any romantic notions that the citizens or council might have utilised these as an urban harvest; he also bemoaned the lack of organic vegetables — this in spite (or even because?!) of fairly healthy food, and radical political, cultures.

So the journey ended, as I had a hunch it might, with a familiar riddle: how to construct the rainbow bridge that should only connect (as EM Forster might have it) our brave crazy human race with food, land, nature, each other…with wonder.

And so, back to the job in hand: a year at the urban market garden.

As promised, I come bearing seed, notably a fine chilli cultivar, "Bolivian Rainbow", courtesy of the Finca Colina Chilli Patch. But seeing the amount of work that has gone on in my absence, I feel more prodigal son than returning hero.

Conference Call

January 25, 2013

A long pause in the Hawkwood blogosphere since the last post over a month ago. Things are moving slowly: the dark still of midwinter has been underscored by the recent deep frosts and down duvets of snow. Steadily, we have got on with the important-but-not-urgent winter tasks: mulching the Entrance Field; digging to extend the Old Kitchen Garden; building raised beds in the glasshouse; and raising the "Alpine Terrace" on the West Bank. There have been some brilliant crisp days, and some biting Siberian winds, enjoyed and endured by all the stalwarts here.

The seed ordering, like the other Yule customs, has come and long gone, and not for the first time so much of the joy was in the anticipation. Desperately trying to finalise the orders by the end of the New Year hangover week, I realised I wasn't exactly living the dream of drawn cosy nights by the fire, sloe gin and time in hand, savouring next year's bounty. Maybe this year.

On the produce front, the salad is at impasse, and our homegrown winter stores boast "only" our vital garlic after the great squash clear out. Rots began to set in before Christmas, and by the New Year it was obvious we had to cut our losses: box scheme members enjoyed what I'd hoped we could drip-feed into the stalls into spring. This squash storage puzzle was one I resolved to get solved at the Organic Producers' Conference in Birmingham this week.

Here, 200 producers, researchers and campaigners huddled into Aston University. As snow fell thick outside, we shared the pain of 2012's weather extremes, and the hopes for agro-ecological futures. The bio-crisis seems to loom ever closer to home, making the task of building resilient food systems appear ever more urgent, and too slow. If it wasn't for the commonwealth of wisdom and compassion you find in these sorts of gatherings, things would look utterly desperate.

Days of exploring seed saving, tool innovations and the emergence of Via Campesina UK; nights of too much organic ale and arguments about endive. In the wee hours, a white fluffy fracas ensued, involving the OrganicLea delegates, the Irish growers and Soil Association staff. If I can't throw snowballs I don't want to be part of your revolution, as Emma almost said.[2]

As for the squash question, I got a few pointers. The answer, though, is howling in the arctic wind, only to be revealed this time next year. In the meantime, the rhubarb is up: the anticipation of a glorious growing season. Today, the forest's woodpeckers competed with Huf's jack hammer to provide the drum roll…

Birds, Floods and Resolutions

January 19, 2014

Returning to Hawkwood after midwinter's Long Pause, I'm relieved to find little wind damage despite the Christmas and Boxing Day Gales. The crop covers had blown clean off the naked brassicas in the Entrance Field (I say "brassicas" as if we grow an extended family of greens, when actually they're all minor variants on the kale theme, such is the present popularity of this ancient superfood), yet no bird damage was evident. This serves as a reminder that wood pigeons are like the rest of us, featheriness and bulging eyes aside: they're creatures of habit, and once they've established their feeding stations it can be surprising for how long they will overlook better dining options right under their beaks.

This was just one theme addressed at the Oxford Real Farming Conference last week, attended by a dozen-strong OrganicLea delegation. Not that of pigeon protection (or not in the sessions I attended at any stretch) but of human habitual behaviour. When asked, a large slice of the population pie want their diet to be more local, organic, community-led, yet when offered this at reasonably competitive prices, many of us manage to switch our shopping habits as swiftly as the proverbial oil tanker.

Which is one of a number of factors coming together to whip up climate change. Climate change, in turn, is one of a number of factors coming together to prise open the floodgates, alongside soil management, increased hard landscape and loss of flood plains. It's not just winter – nowadays it seems like a week doesn't go by in Britain without some poor village somewhere getting flushed out of their homes – but in another example of human limitations, I tend to consider things more when they are right in my face. The Thames had burst into Oxford city centre as the Real Farming Conference[3], and its "business as usual" counterpart, the Oxford Farming Conference, proceeded; and back at Hawkwood every bit of ground is thoroughly waterlogged, and new springs spring forth.

Maybe it comes from approaching middle age, but lately I find the most uplifting moments come in weather-beaten. In a field blistered with puddles, the resilience of the red radicchio is fortifying. The small supergreen shoots of overwintering garlic, and the swelling rose buds of rhubarb, are enough to bring a tear to the eye. Yet even these purest of gifts, the ability to gaze on harbingers of spring, are not always without conflict. It's been a very wet, very mild winter, and I'd sooner see a decent cold snap to knock back pest and disease and make the temperate plants feel more at home. If the last decade is anything to go by, winter and summer tend to mirror each other: bright cold winter followed by bright warm summer, mild damp leading to mild damp. Time will tell its own tale.

On reflection, "natural purity", untainted by worries such as climate change and flooding, is an ideal we can never realise. The Earth is awesome, wonderful, terrifying, messy, dirty and gorgeous, and humans are of her and crawl over her. Perfection is beyond us, but still, there is scope to behave in ways — and push for social institutions — that facilitate a more kindly, sharing, lighter presence on the planet. As we are still in the time of resolutions, let's plump for some of these.

Outside Inside

January 28, 2014

"When a great ship is in harbour and moored, it is safe, there can be no doubt. But…that is not what great ships are built for."- Clarissa Estes[4]

> *"And smoke never lies, in truth*
> *it's better outside, but the proof*
> *took time, took spring to mix water colours, took*
> *summer for the land to laugh out land again."*
> *- Ru Litherland, "Outside Inside" (1999)[5]*

Whilst the general synopsis for this winter is, thus far: mild; alternately damp and soaking; and firmly on the miserable spectrum, there have nonetheless been some glorious days in the garden. In last week's afternoons we and the sleeping beautiful plants were bathed in that base gold limelight that only comes through this season's narrow window. I tend to associate it with those dramatic, sharp, frost-tinted January moments, but am glad to recount that even in the absence of freezing temperatures, being caught in that grace gifts you the sense that the Great Outdoors is the greatest place to be.

That said, the indoor environment, now at the limit of its annual swing from stuffy to cosy, is currently a delight too. Jonny and I have been pulling beetroot out of the sheltered store: denuded of leaves but as firm and vibrantly flushing as when we tore them from the Entrance Field tilth on that bustling T-shirted Harvest Day at the end of September. That's the power of clamps: an ancient method, rather than fixed design, of storing root crops in the off-season. In harmony with everything else here, our clamps are a late urban twist on rustic tradition, fabricated with branded builders' sacks, pallets and coconut fibre in place of field trenches and straw. Clamps don't have to be indoors, but ours are: specifically, in the Ambient House, as we have dubbed the cool storage section of the building.

This is the first year of the Ambient and its attendant clamps. It was constructed as part of a significant building development that we embarked on after confirming our thirty-year lease. The works also included the decommissioning of the oil-fired boilers, the installation of a walk-in chiller, and the creation of the Beetroot Office (where the distribution and infrastructure workers are clamped), in a programme called, somewhat uninspiringly, "Building Phase Two", as the Maoists already had dibs on "The Great Leap Forward" and "Let A Thousand Salad Leaves Unfold"[6].

So presently the greater weight of produce emanates from the Ambient House rather than directly from the ground. From there we've moved most of our squash mountain, and garlic and potatoes trickle onto the Farm Stall. Meanwhile inside the House of Glass there is much movement: storage systems are overhauled, capillary sand replaced, pots and trays sorted, glass washed, preparations made for new beds and vent maintenance.

It's the spaces in between that are often the most interesting, and it's exactly on the threshold between in and out that Theo, our new-ish Site Development Worker, seems to spend much of his time: installing cabins for firewood logs, and erecting the peach protection frame against the glasshouse, which will keep all this dirty British drizzle off our fine Mediterranean friends. It's painted a fitting Italian azzurro: it's functional and beautiful. Around the corner, against the East Glasshouse "wall", he's engineered a hardening bench, a brilliant development that will dramatically reduce the damage to our plants during that critical week in the halfway house between the "intensive care unit" that is the propagation area, and the cold beyond-the-pale light of day Out There: the wild soils, the uncertain wind- and slug- swept shores; the manhandling of the commutes through our plant stalls.

After the builders, the gardeners: we've laid down the capillary, the black geotextile "floor", and set out hardy green plants in a semblance of order. And it looks, we look, to all intents and purposes, like a proper plant nursery. Looking at it, no visitor would guess that, indoors or outdoors, we're just playing.

February

First Fruit

February 12, 2010

On the one hand, spring comes silently, like snow. Bulbs begin to peer over the parapet and buds seem slightly plumper, but there's no visible growth in the garden, even under glass. The end of winter is played in slow motion.

On the other hand, the birds are going bananas.

February is not many people's favourite month. Maybe I see it differently because it contains my birthday, or maybe it's because February is, on a good day, the last chance to experience the heart-aching winter light, and to see it more, teased out with the lengthening days.

Friday was the first "Fruity Friday": from now on, every Friday here at Hawkwood will be devoted to work around fruit. After the flailing, mowing and slashing of bramble to make way for the beginnings of the vineyard, I leant on the scythe and looked out over wooded Yardley Hill, drinking in the range of understated hues displayed by naked trees.

The vineyard is in a good spot. It is in "zone 2" of the site, further away from base camp (the tool shed and kitchen) than the vegetables which require more regular attention. Marko, the viticulturalist, reckons that it might even be the warmest spot on the site: it's more sheltered than most, whilst still being open. He's noticed that the deer – with whom we hope to strike an entente cordial with regard to which plants they eat – sit just down the slope, in what is to be the "traditional orchard" for late season apples.

These are long-term projects: it'll be five years before we get a decent crop off either vines or apple trees: they are as twinkles in our eyes. The promise of fruit for this year came in an unpromising brown package at the end of the day: fifty autumn raspberry canes: small, weedy, muddied and snoozing, oblivious to the great expectations placed on them, the anticipated first fruits of our labours.

Hard Play

February 20, 2010

It has been a bitter, sun-scarce winter; fortunately there's been plenty of physical graft here to keep the circulation pumping. Somewhere amidst all the shovelling, trenching, digging, posting and lifting I've developed a nagging muscle strain. I'm not sure if it's a bicep or tricep, as it's never been conspicuous enough to be positively identified. Whichever, it meant that this week I was made to assume the unsung "holding" role whilst Annie and Little Ru (one of two Rus at Hawkwood, an above average demographic) had the pain/pleasure of driving "rustic" poles three foot into the solid clay, the last post in a long hard sweet chestnut journey.

It began with an innocent enquiry to Adrian Leaman at Wholewoods Environmental Arts[7]. Wholewoods – Adrian and his trusty sidekick Kath – has done with wood what OrganicLea has done with vegetables: that is, taken wood, woodlands and related issues (sustainable building, timber, tools) back into the desert of London with determination, flair and a little lunacy. By the time of the conversation, they had felled a little bit of London and pulled it into the Ashdown Forest, from where they run courses and events that reconnect people and trees.

At OrganicLea we've spent years helping reconnect people and food, by disconnecting, in various ways, from the destructive industrial system of food production and distribution. But much of a garden's "hard landscape" is dependent on equally destructive industrial processes, such as tree plantations, wood treating and cement making. With this in mind, I asked Adrian if he could suggest a source of local, sustainably produced hardwood for fence posts for the St. Pauli[8] garden in Hackney.

The next thing I know, I'm in darkest Sussex sawing down trees in our "Adopt-a-Coppice" scheme. It's a profoundly simple scheme whereby we manage a portion of woodland in return for its product. So the chestnut poles have been sawn, pulled up a muddy slope, bundled in and out of a van, pointed and shaved, and now driven into the entrance field, all by our own fair hands, where they will fulfil their purpose of:

a) supporting espaliered fruit trees;

b) supporting a wire mesh fence in the event of deer or even rabbits proving a problem for vegetable cultivation on the field.

After all that, you begin to have a relationship with these odd bits of wood stuck in the ground. They promise to stay true and I have promised to adorn them with pear blossom. Mind, you can never be sure how relationships are going to pan out.

Potato Dreaming

February 24, 2010

I have a fond memory, a memory I fondle like a childhood, of sowing tomato seeds in a glasshouse while it snowed outside. We haven't got any toms in yet, which is a sore point I won't pick at, but on Monday I arrived, having cycled up the River Lea against a northerly blizzard, to find Clare's gardening class setting out potatoes to chit.

You feel slightly foolish doing it: it feels like an act of faith rather than experience: in fact it's both.

The weather – not the occasional pretty snow, but the relentless gloom and damp – is getting me down, so let's turn to potatoes. At one point in my life, I thought I'd never grow them again: too much of a "farmers' crop": cheap and cheerful, economically viable only if you work in fields and tractors, not with gardens and trowels. But now, with twelve acres…well, they won't keep us in jobs, but they will vigorously break up the ground in the fresh field, and suppress opportunist weeds. So, spuds have returned, and it's a wonderful world.

This year we have Pentland Javelin as a disease resistant first early; Milva as the second early, which has triumphed in organic taste and yield tests; and Arran Victory, an old (1918) blue-skinned late maincrop from the great Isle of Arran stable. They chit now, and soon they will look outstanding with their tall broad leaves, dainty yellow-beaked flowers, and their cool firm tubers drawn from the earth like nuggets of gold. Except for the blue ones.

There is a pleasure to be had from growing, harvesting, eating potatoes that feels almost primordial, which is deceptive given that on this island we've only cultivated them with any enthusiasm for the last couple of centuries or so.

There's something very, very primordial about algae and moss though: they are the pioneers in the conversion of water and rock to soil, the very foundation of life. Truly awesome, but sometimes you want to slow down even that slow process for a bit, like when they are starting to nibble away at the half an acre of glasshouse you've just inherited.

My Top Tip for moss and algae removal from glasshouses is to hold out for a really miserable, chilling wet winter's day, when the only sensible place to be is inside the glasshouse; then borrow a pressure washer and spray it around until you're quite shivering from the "great outdoors" experience. Then console yourself with the thought that what you're doing is not so much an act of faith as one of denial: ultimately these simple organisms will take the glasshouse, "paving" the way for scrubby succession. Better enjoy those potato moments while we still can.

Letter from Americas

February 1, 2011

There's been over a month's lull since the last posting, reflecting a rest in my horticultural activity. Much as we all love summer holidays, late December/ January is for many growers the ideal time to kick back or disappear: after all, that is what the plants are doing. Usually, I take this time to make local, and inner, journeys. This year, though, I lit the carbon bullet and went transatlantic.

In the high density of New York I witnessed the unstoppable human urge to cultivate: micro-allotments on rescued strips of land, market gardens (or "urban farms" as they like to call them) on roof tops, reclaimed ball courts, and an unoccupied island! Urban agriculture is fairly advanced in the US in general, buoyed by the popularity of farmers' markets[9]. Good news, but with it, inevitably, come challenges. For instance, how to respond when a pioneering urban farmer is elevated to celebrity status, and does a deal with Wal-Mart, who surely represent everything community food production isn't? An early warning for local and organic food citizens here in Blighty.

In Mexico I've seen, for the first time with adult eyes, the sheer fecundity of rainforest: how plants there jostle for every conceivable, and inconceivable, bit of space and light. In the highlands of Chiapas there was Extreme Farming – maize fields rotating through mountain banks I would think too steep to set foot on, let alone garden. Fittingly, some of these "milpas" also displayed good examples of the renowned Mayan "Three Sisters" polyculture of corn, squash and beans.

In the Mexican cities, it was back yard fruit trees that flew the flag for "productive" plants, whilst the food culture – always underscored by one or more of the numerous types of chilli pepper – is scintillating.

Some of these chilli types, recipes and growing techniques I will attempt to introduce and adapt to our cool island setting; some will simply not make sense here, but will live on as a memory, a dream. Ultimately, I defer to Proust: "the real voyage of discovery consists not in seeking new lands but in seeing with new eyes". This is the best reason for going away: to return with a refreshed perspective on this island, this patch of earth. I can report that it is fertile; green; lush; and, if you look closely, you can see it is just stirring into life.

On Plants and People

February 13, 2011

Sometimes plants and soil are but a peripheral part of what's going on here. On Friday, it was almost a surprise to find myself planting the second wave of raspberries on Raspberry Row. Over the last week I've been immersed in all manner of admin, meetings, teaching and recruitment. But this is what it means to be a grower on an urban community market garden, managed by a workers' cooperative, worked by volunteers. Not for nothing is Hawkwood Nursery's strapline "for plants and people".

On balance, I wouldn't have it any other way. Without people, communities, along the road back to nature we'd all get lost. Sure, as a result the land won't be as productive in crops as a purely commercial venture. But the age of maximum productivity is, as we are seeing, terminal. The task now is surely to approach the optimum. And this entails some sort of fine balance between the social, the economical, and the ecological.

The raspberries are another autumn cultivar, the classic "Autumn Bliss". Nothing against summer raspberries, but we're hoping that strawberries will become our "summer fruit". I like the idea of the "fruit of the season" title being graciously passed on, uncontested, through the year, as well as the practicalities of focused attention and harvesting. Fruit isn't too much work, except when it's fruiting. This is not as much an example of Sod's Law as it sounds, because work isn't as hard as it sounds.

Last year's raspberries are showing swelling green buds already, so we're late pruning: the growing season hasn't started, and we're already behind! It's time to delay some admin and get out there...

Kings of Spring

February 22, 2011

There has been a lot of action in the glasshouses lately: pots and labels have been sorted, potting benches swept so clean you could sow your dinner on them. Ed and Sonny have done their time breaking the stone floor, to let some more earth shine through. It's looking ship-shape, I thought to myself, but a little, I don't know, bare. Like something was missing. Then I realised what: plants.

Not everyone's first choice for the conservatory, I admit, but when I fetched in a trolley of potted rhubarb, they really lifted the place. The stems are already a few inches tall, with the blush vividity of only youth, and wee leaves unclenching as prettily as a flower bud. THIS is what makes perennials – especially herbaceous perennials – great: they are ahead of the game. We will be picking rhubarb outside while the courgette seeds are still snoring in their tins.

I didn't just bring the crowns in to make the place look elegant, though. Next week's Open Day at Hawkwood is our unilaterally-declared Rhubarb Day, a celebration of this fine spring fruit. Our answer to the famous forcing sheds of Yorkshire is the Cockney Blanching Bender in the Kitchen Garden, from under which we will pluck choice pink "champagne" stalks for sale and tastings. The latter will be in the form of "sherbet dips", that confectionary product apparently being inspired by rhubarb stems dabbed in sugar.

Elsewhere, we planted half an orchard last week, and got the post and wire ready for the espaliered pears and cooking apples. We live in the faith that someone, somewhere, is growing us some oats: the economic future is crumble.

Cold Hands Warm Glow

February 5, 2012

This week I've lain in bed shivering, but have been warmed by the heat waves of grim satisfaction that accompanies a hard cold snap.

Gardeners in particular like a spell of ice. Traditionally round here, they'd expose clay clods to the frost's shattering forces. Organic practitioners abhor a bare soil in winter, but see Jack Frost as an ally in killing off key pests such as slugs and aphids. There's also the notion that a "proper" winter begets a "proper" summer, one that recent patterns would appear to confirm.

At Hawkwood, the restart of salad picking has been put on hold, and the glasshouse taps have burst. Digging work is slow in the morning as spades have to break soil hard as stone before getting in to the soft underbelly, to remove perennial weeds or make trenches for raspberries.

But these winter curses are offset by the aforementioned gardeners' delight, the joy of the crisp fresh days of golden light, and a widened window for fruit planting and pruning. Mary, our new Veg & Fruit worker, will be grateful indeed for this, given the complex and diverse plans she has inherited.

These include the speculative planting of almonds, which I heeled in on Friday, dreaming all the while of the pink-white honeyed marzipan blossom I walked amongst but two weeks ago in Andalucia. There, I was told, they didn't have a winter, more like two springs. All well and good for southern Spain, but amongst the terrible fears for climate change is the psycho-culturally deep one, that our planet's rich diversity of seasonal rhythms will be eroded: bland capitalist monoculture creating a global weather system after its own image.

To which the hushed notes of the falling snow reply, give us cold toes but give us parsnips.

Under the Concrete

February 13, 2012

In a week where a nation skidded into "snow chaos", and even the mighty Stevenage FC declared their frozen ground unplayable, I am proud to report that a quorate Hawkwood crew carried on gardening.

Digging in the Old Kitchen Garden continued apace, leaving a rich black slice set in the driven white, a sight that resembled a giant Christmas cake or megapint of stout, and was equally as cheering. The only patches of land not covered to ankle-level are those under cover, the glasshouse and the garage/ workshop, and here there's been much brisk activity.

The council concreted most of the half-acre of land under glass: their operation was all about containerised plants for shipping out to bloom the borough. Two years into our occupation, and it looks like our requirements are the reverse: a relatively small proportion of the glasshouse is used for propagation, even though we raise thousands of plants for sale; whereas any amount of vegetables grown under glass, in the Lea Valley tradition, seem to be well-received by our members, partners and customers. Each winter, we chip away at the cement face, opening up more ground.

Having broken rock, this week we rolled away the last of the boulders standing in the way of this year's six new veg beds. More milestones. It felt like the right moment to turn to Paco, our Parisian migrant worker, and mutter that fine slogan of the May '68 Rising "Sous le pave, la plage" (under the pavement, the beach). Revolutionary spirit dented, but not defeated, by having my pronunciation corrected, I considered the act of returning hard landscape to soil, to plants: an alternative model of regeneration, and a highly symbolic and satisfying one, wherever it is performed. The OrganicLea logo features a boot and garden spade lifting a paving slab. This image was scrumped (with their blessing) from an Adbusters image of the same tool going through a Safeway (remember them?) supermarket. The dream of a return to the land exploding the nightmare of soullessness.

The natural magic of snow might temporarily mask the cold hardness of our architecture, but in all times and all places there waits, under the concrete, the earth.

Sievings of Spring

February 26, 2012

On Tuesday, trudging up to the Old Kitchen Garden for more winter digging, my thermal undergarments hung distinctly heavy on me. The earliest of early weeds, cleavers, or sticky willy as he's known to his friends, was cagily creeping across the soil surface. With the dry weather forecast on our side, we had a hoe down on the rows of broad beans. And spring was in my step: whether it was the amplified bird song, a subtle tone change in the forest that embraces and bleeds into the site; or the minute vibrations of sap rising around us, I don't know. All I know is that thick-thin rush pulsing up through me: growth is returning.

The plants that have hunched with us through a hard winter are beginning to stretch yawningly, first in the glasshouse, then al fresco. In the former, the rocket is already bolting. Even the escarole, which for the last few months has been complaining that it would rather have been left at home on the Med in the first place, is starting to look less sorry for itself.

The day came to a glorious close with a second planting of broad beans, on the extended perimeters of the garden: a kidney-shaped full stop on cold days spent chipping away at the bramble knuckles.

Despite its infinite wisdom, even nature makes false starts sometimes, and some of the weather prophets are still talking of a returning Siberian snap. But here at Hawkwood, we know it is time to dust down the potting benches: when our elders, Ken and Brian, start sieving leaf mould, it is a sure sign that the seed sowing season is upon us.

Miracle-Grow

February 6, 2013

"You have to know the difference/ Between the roundabouts and swings/ No matter what the distance/ Winter turns to spring."- Robb Johnson, Winter Turns to Spring[10]

Winter is not yet passed: indeed, another freezy spell is on its way; yet there are glimmers now, and the odd miracle. On the West Bank Terrace it plummeted to minus twelve degrees in the Big Chill. Venturing out this week to pay witness to the wreckage in its wake, it was a shock to find a full bed of leaf celery pushing energetically against its tidy fleece. A thin fleece, small protection for such tender stems. I can only imagine that the act of care in clothing the plants gave them some extra spur of encouragement to stick it out.

Our early encouragement is provided by the perennials, as ever. On the salad beds, the chives and burnet are already looking pretty lively, while around the place hawthorn buds crouch and hazel catkins purr. Temperature is, after all, only one part of the equation: day length is another. We are now closer to the spring equinox than the winter solstice, and the plants know it. The first pea flower was out on Tuesday.

We have entertained Jack Frost and the Wild Western Wind at Hawkwood this last month, both bringing their particular brand of joy and havoc, but neither have done much to dry out the soaking fields. I have never known the place so wet for so long. The paths have lapsed into drawn-out puddles, and the cultivated soil is, or rather should be, off bounds to human tread, to prevent further structural damage.

Spring always comes burdened with heavy expectations, and its possible promise of a warm drying spell is the current great white hope. It's a hope glimmering like a miracle some distance away yet; after all, spring is what hope does.

Nor Shall My Spade Sleep in My Hand

February 13, 2011

In recent times, I have been encouraging people to sing Blake's "Jerusalem" whilst planting or harvesting Jerusalem artichokes. And so, on Wednesday, a distinctly un-angelic version of the hymn fell from the upper echelons of the Old Kitchen Garden, as the red-skinned tubers were troweled into the cold ground.

"Alternative national anthem" it may be, but my research shows – when it comes to that section of society who plant artichokes – that over half don't know the tune, and of those that do, half of them don't get it. These facts don't make for a great choral recital; but listen: very few vegetables have their own theme tune, so why waste a rare opportunity?

For those of you in the majority camp, let me explain that in this song William Blake, the eighteenth-century London mystic, juxtaposes the spectre of pollution and suffering of the industrial age with an imagined golden era when Jesus rambled round England's pleasant pastures showering blessings, and "the countenance divine/ [shone] forth upon our clouded hills". He goes on to commit himself mentally and physically to struggle to build Jerusalem – the Promised Land – "in England's green and pleasant land". Stirring stuff, but what the onions has it got to do with gardening?

As in so much poetry and prose, the natural world, and the stewarded natural world, are presented as a vision of redemption in a landscape where people are incarcerated in "dark satanic mills". Such was the scene in our industrial cities then. If Billy Blake is watching now, he'll see the smoky factories have merely been relocated to other, exotic, locations. For us, the work may now be less "dirty", but drudgery and alienation remain the order of the day. And the same push-pull factors that prised the English peasant from their pleasant pastures and mountains green to fill the filthy city streets remain in full operation. As reported in the winter issue of *The Land*, the global financial and resource crisis has sparked off a "land rush", with governments and multinationals buying up vast tracts of "underutilised" agricultural soil, for industrial agriculture and mining: vast numbers of people are being slung off their farms and gardens. They are taking with them their ancient feet, their holy lambs. History is repeating itself, tragically. At Hawkwood, as in community gardens across the urban scene, we see the burning desire to return to the garden.

But what the parsnips has this all got to do with Jerusalem artichokes? Well, precious little, it must be conceded. Their connection to the literal or conceptual Old City is tenuous indeed. A Native American crop, they arrived in Europe in the early seventeenth century. Their name stems from a misunderstanding, intentional or otherwise. If you ignore the gardening books and let them flower, you'll see the resemblance to their close relative the sunflower. So the Italians named it as they named the sunflower, girasol, after the flower's habit of turning to the sun. Another theory posits the bastardisation of Ter Neusen, the area in the Netherlands where the tuber was originally introduced to Europe.

The name may be an apparent accident of diction, but maybe not: they are by no means an inappropriate plant to carry Blake's ode to hope. They are planted in the dark times, even in the snow, as we did last week. For us they are the first plantings of the unborn growing season, premature harbingers of spring, that green and pleasant land in waiting. From there, they rise up, and up: as tall as a tree, in a season, following the sun, eyes on the prize.

This week, clouds unfold. The first salad harvest; the tomatoes are sown. Bring me my wheelbarrow of desire.

Dark Skies, Shooting Stars of Crumble

February 12, 2014

"What good is land without its bit of encircling sky?" asks Gill Baron, koan-like, in this winter's issue of *The Land*[11]. Our piece of sky here at Hawkwood can't rival the Big Blue of the East Anglian plains, at whose centre our partners Hughes Organics stand; nor the distant hillside panoramas that cradle so many "Back-to-the-Landers", but it's ours, special and wonderful in its own way, and at this time of year it's as wide and open as it gets.

The loss of leaf canopy all round sees the trees throwing starker shapes, and expands the aerial environment surprisingly, stretching it out past the old hornbeam pollards as far as Yates' Meadow to the north, and over the reservoirs to the grey and glass rises of Ponders End and Freezy Water, now districts of Enfield both, to the west. In between, more space and time. It's a phenomena that I believe is known to that section of people who don't actually live in urban river basins as a "view". Not much call for it round 'ere.

Another atmospheric feature that us folk in The Smoke find equally splendid but unnervingly agoraphobia-inducing is something they call "the stars". On a clear night we're lucky enough to get the odd twinkle here in the Darkness On The Edge Of Town, but the Milky Way is drowned in the street lamp glow and retail glitz, and with it that valuable reminder of our tiny place in the universe. A profound loss. It's the oral exclamations of the creatures that claim the space when home time comes for Hawkwood workers, that we rely on to tell us we're not alone here: the rutting deer, the wailing fox, the questioning owl. And our sowing and planting schedule is directed by the lunar cycle, so we know when it's a waxing moon even when we can't spot its light shed.

Globally, the International Dark Sky Association campaigns for people's right to starlight, and has declared parts of this island, among them the Brecon Beacons, Exmoor and Galloway Forest, as "International Dark Sky Parks" – islands of low light pollution. Doubtless I'd get short odds on East London being one of the last areas to achieve such status, but a small patch of our site now has its perpetual black ceiling on: the "Cockney Blanching Benders" are now over the Timperly Early rhubarb, removing their light for a couple of moons so as to yield, from next week, "champagne rhubarb". The pink stems of which are so prized, in the past for an early source of fresh fruity vitamins; in the now for its tender, sweeter, melt-in-the-mouth quality.

As much as it is welcomed, there are understandable mixed feelings about this "veal of the vegetable world". Undoubtedly, the blanching process stresses the plant, though the work of the gardener is to stress it but not stress it out. And this rhubarb race, like the humans that grow it and eat it, is anaemic, fatigued, pale from constantly stretching for the sky, the stars beyond. Yet from these tortuous tunnels come patterns of great beauty, hope in the darkness, new forms of delicacy.

And the best kind of crumble.

New from Old

February 24, 2014

"Another world is not only possible, she is on her way. On a quiet day, I can hear her breathing."
- *Arundhati Roy*

This week the smell of spring is unmistakable. A mild surprise, as there's not been a "real" winter. There's been plenty of weather alright, but that's not quite the same thing. We've held back from resuming our weekly salad deliveries — they can only restart once a year — on the guesstimate that, going on recent times, this land and its flora will be held in an icy grip at some point. If Jack Frost is still planning a visit, his fashionable lateness is now way beyond cool: crocuses are out, the dawn chorus is tuning up, and the overwintering rocket is going to flower, its frost protection fleece lying crumpled, barely worn, at its feet. It's time we begun.

There is a freshness to everything now: the resinous waft of the wood chip mulch laid down to protect the soft fruit; the clean slate of the black bare of just-planted artichoke bed; the annual tidiness of the propagation benches. The ol' garden is, of a sudden, new. This is The Thing about gardening: resurrection is not a utopia or a religious belief: it's an event. It happens once a year in a big way, with small revolutions occurring every month, week, day…

This month, in our crooked corner of this built-up city, I will be one of the thousands of new gardeners sowing new seeds. There are old and new volunteers helping to rekindle the growing season at Hawkwood, where our latest attractions include Jerusalem Drive, the Walthamstow Yellow Cress Welcome Bed, and an exploding World of Chillies. Some of these will join the hundreds more across the borough that now have access to an allotment.

Waltham Forest has created 200 new food-growing plots in the last year, and reduced the allotment waiting list dramatically, as part of its Food Growing Strategy. A lot more people are talking about food growing now, but as yet few local authorities have seen fit to exercise their statutory powers in support of local production. I am proud of Waltham Forest, and OrganicLea's small part in effecting the zeitgeist and the political will.

It's time to get out there, effect small changes. Create the new garden, either literally, turning run-off hard landscape into a porous plant paradise, a flood of relief[12]; or reclaiming and redeeming the battered waste ground which last year you once grew. And from that garden we climb, tendril by curly tendril, onwards and outwards: conversations over the allotment fence; swapping seeds with the world at the community garden; walking straight past Tesco with community-grown, wildlife-friendly veg. Gardens are a retreat from the world, and also a reconstruction of it — a springboard to a redeemed economy based on nature and nurture, to a renewed architecture — beautiful, socially useful. Worms turn, badger crossings, land liberated.

   Time to pick up the trowel you threw in last Winter of Discontent, and Dig In for victory.

"Whether you have never gardened before in your life, or are a gardener of fifty years' standing, makes no difference: stop reading this and get outside. Happy new garden."
- *Monty Don*

March

Onto the Streets (2010)
Our weekly market stall selling fruit and vegetables, bread, jams and plants,
on the corner of Bakers Avenue / Hoe Street, Walthamstow

You Say Tomato

March 6, 2010

We've made it.

The season has started. In one week, we have witnessed a fundamental change of gear and perspective, from the broad strokes of the climate and landscape, to tiny seeds sown into three centimetre modules. In one week we have a twenty-four metre propagation bench lined, wired and gravelled up, and sown with subtropical "fruiting vegetables". Most importantly, we have embarked on the next chapter of the Kondine Red story.

The story begins with my granddad. Granddad Fred is one of the heroes in my life, someone who, in my own way, I've drawn much inspiration from: someone who is not afraid of holding unconventional views and sticking by them, and someone who loved to work on the land. For him, as for me, these two things came together at one point in his life: as a conscientious objector during the Second World War, he was put onto land service, and spent the war working in the fields of Essex.

During the war effort, tomatoes were regarded as an important vegetable crop in terms of nutritional value per area, so much so that they were grown on a field scale. Fred recalls spending days on end going up and down rows pinching out, and going to bed seeing tomato row after tomato row as he shut his eyelids. "The best times of my life", he'd later say.

As my horticultural interest developed, I asked my granddad if he could remember which varieties of tomato he used to work with. "Kondine Red" he answered without hesitation: "[the farmer] said it was the only tomato that would grow well in the Essex soil". By this time I was gardening in Hackney, not too far from "the Essex soil", and I quite fancied the idea of growing "my Granddad's tomato" in our glasshouses.

So I flicked through a few seed catalogues without success. The ever-reliable Google search found few references to Kondine Red, and these referred to a past scientific trial: no one was offering to sell me any. I visited the Heritage Seed Library[13], who coordinate the living seed bank of old and threatened vegetable varieties, but to no avail: even their thousands-strong database did not list this once important cultivar.

The last hope was the self-same Heritage Seed Library's Annual Catalogue, where they not only list seeds available to members, but also host a Seed Swap page, where members list what seeds they have spare and what they're searching for. (A large gene pool of seed is now illegal to sell, so such schemes, and the gift economy, are the only guarantor of our rich vegetable biodiversity.)

Not long after the Catalogue came out, I received a small package from one Del Marcangelo of Ruislip, containing two small batches of the legendary tomato seed. We've made it. According to Del, the variety originated in 1931: *Mr. Cuthbert's Guide to Growing Tomatoes* (1953) declared it "a short-jointed variety and a heavy cropper.

One of the best-known and most popular types", whilst in 1962 *Carter's Tested Seeds* Blue Book described it as "a prolific cropper of good quality fruit". Yet by the end of the century Kondine had become, apparently, all but extinct. The world of vegetables is as fast moving and fickle as any other, so it appears.

The seeds germinated, and by August we were cropping Granddad Fred's conscientious love apple in our Springfield Garden. This would almost qualify as a horticultural fairy tale, but for one final twist: these "Dig For Victory" heroes didn't grow that well in our sub-Essex soil, and didn't taste of much.

But such considerations can't be allowed to get in the way of a good story: in the intervening years I've carried on growing Kondine Red and saving seed: the plant has adapted better to our soil now, and I do believe we've started to breed more flavour back into it: quite unprompted, a friend of mine who bought a number of tomato plants from us a couple of years ago voted KR as his number one for yield and flavour.

As I write, they are starting to stir in our hand-mixed seed compost, on our fresh gravel bench, in our brave new glasshouses. There is still a peace to be won. I have a feeling this will be their year.

Springs and Spirals

March 18, 2010

Nine years ago last month, a bunch of people came together, calling themselves OrganicLea, to "sustainably rehabilitate the food growing heritage of the Lea Valley". Their first steps on this mission were communal work days to clear overgrown plots at Hawkwood allotments, Chingford, for cultivation of organic fruit and vegetables, for themselves and the wider community.

I think back to those pioneering days now, as myself and Nicole, both of us present "at the birth", once again embark on clearing an almost infinite swathe of tenacious bramble. Nine years on, we've inched five minutes up the road to this old council nursery site, in order to start again. Life does indeed go in spirals: gladly this is an upward and outward one.

In 2001, we started work with a few begged and borrowed tools, a small pot of cash raised from a benefit, on a site with no infrastructure but running water. We had a few enthusiastic friends and volunteers, and a world to win.

To paraphrase Durruti, the new world is [still] in our hearts, and it is growing this minute[14]. The last decade has witnessed a surge of interest in organic and local food production, and community gardens have mushroomed. OrganicLea is now an established workers' cóoperative with staff and firm roots in this corner of east London, based on a range of past and present projects and activities, including the market stall and box scheme, and the renowned "scrumping project". On the strength of all the above, the council offered us a ten-year lease on Hawkwood Plant Nursery (or Hawkwood Nursery for Plants and People, to give it its full title), a 12-acre site bordering Epping Forest, with purpose-built glasshouses and buildings, in which to scale up local production of food, food plants, and training.

Given all this, it is suitably grounding to be back to bashing scrub. And even the bashing has an upward spiral to it: back in the day, not knowing or affording any better, we used loppers, secateurs and sickles; Nicole claims she even resorted to scissors to attack the great blackberry trunks! Today, we have equipment specifically engineered for the job: Sean loves the Irish slasher, while I lean towards the Austrian scythe with the "Fux" bramble blade. Then we go in with the flail mower, and the roots are finally dug out with a mattock, which (as the rest of the world has known for some time) makes relatively light work of such a task compared to the spade, which we and every other English gardener persisted in using at the start of this century.

So, as we approach the spring equinox and its brief perfect balance between light and dark, let's drink to spirals: onwards and outwards.

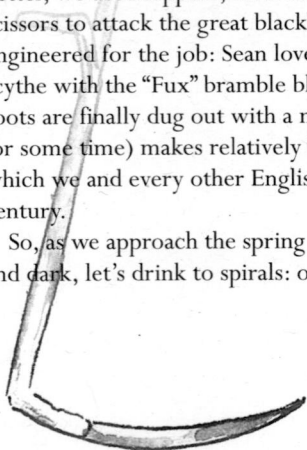

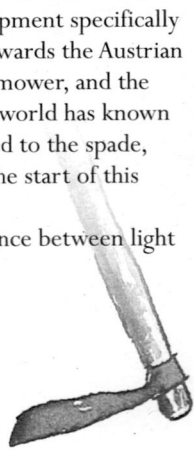

I'm So Excited

March 24, 2010

I spent most of the weekend in and around the glasshouse. On Saturday morning I cut five budding daffodils and placed them in a Hackney Wine Vase (beer glass), and from the corner of my eye watched their smiles broaden to beaming grins as we met the spring equinox.

Our early tender friends – tomatoes, peppers, french beans – are germinating well and laying out their leaves with some confidence. The peas have taken everything winter has thrown at them and are coming up snow-white flowers. The first salad seedlings – lettuce, beetroot, sorrel, wild rocket – are rooting through their containers into the gravel: time to get out there. We will have them hardening off next week (note to self: sort out hardening bay irrigation). A big push on Tuesday saw us dig and build the first phase of raised beds on the West Bank Terrace, so we're just about on schedule.

There is this nervous excitement everywhere, oozing up from the ground. Everything – buds, bulbs, birds, bees and bumbling gardeners – is striking out and taking risks. Butterflies in my stomach are sleepless. Yet the things I normally do to divert myself from becoming too obsessed with growing plants – Stevenage Borough FC, road cycling, relationships – all seem similarly teetering on the terrifying brink between glory and, well, glorious failure.

Once the butterflies can be seen fluttering in abundance about the fields here, they will no longer be in my tummy: the anticipation will be becoming actualised. The plants will be out of the nursery and growing up, or at least surviving, in the school of soil life, Mother Earth willing; and everything else in the garden, and in life, will unfold in its own sweet way: it'd be greedy to ask for much more than that.

Seeds

March 2, 2011

We've had a good month of mild weather now, with temperatures not dropping below freezing and plenty of hours above the magic six degree threshold. The first timid suggestion of new leaf from the crops and wild things here at Hawkwood are now turning towards confident renewal, and this is reflected faithfully in the Nursery turning its mind and sights to the growing season ahead.

The latest stage of the glasshouse reorganisation is not quite complete, but like so much in life it will never reach full completion: it has made it to the next base, and that's enough. Now the seed sowing can begin in earnest: as is the custom in these parts, tomatoes were given pole position, to test out the new plug trays.

This year we'll be growing a plethora of tomato cultivars for sale as plants to local gardeners, but for produce we will focus on medium-sized "salad" tomatoes – the English classic, if you will. By way of a twist, these will come in three different colours: striped red/ yellow, in the form of "Tiger Tom"; the yellow "Golden Queen"; and the red "Essex Wonder". We will concentrate our heritage efforts on the latter while giving "Kondine Red" a year's well-deserved rest.

Essex Wonder may well have been bred in the Lea Valley bioregion: it was certainly widely grown here in the area's Tomato Age (1930–1950s), before London looked further afield for its vegetables, causing the decline of market gardens here. So sharp was this little tomato's fall from popularity that it, like the Kondine, became virtually extinct. It only exists now after some eagle-eyed person found three seeds in a tobacco tin in an old allotment shed. From these, with the help of the Heritage Seed Library, the Essex has been brought back to life.

"From small seeds big trees grow", goes the saying. In the metaphorical sense, it is a good time to be thinking about the small things we can do to effect wider change in the world around us; in the literal sense, I'm hoping these small seeds grow modest sized tomatoes, not a bloody forest, in the glasshouse.

By Nature?

March 16, 2011

Perhaps the defining principle of organic gardening is "work with nature, not against it". The extreme opposite of this might be seen to be agro-industry's genetic modification and vast monocultures: gimungous resources – human, environmental, economic – poured into fighting against the nature of things, with inevitably toxic results all round. At the other end of the spectrum, wildlife gardening, foraging, and forest gardens demonstrate that letting things be, with a few timely interventions, can generate riches beyond the dreams of the maximisers.

For the organic grower attempting to produce for the wider community, there is the question of how far we can stray from the latter ideal of beautiful simplicity before we lose our way and stray into the barren mindscape.

Last week I was tying in fan-trained peaches, while inside the trickle irrigation ran and I tried to trick tomatoes, by means of an electric cable, into germinating before time. These are the kind of things that disappoint visitors hoping to find a state-of-nature permaculture project.

On the other hand, peering through the glass I could see the newly established lacewing hotels built by Whitehall schoolchildren, the calendula flowers rising from the predator strips; and the woodpeckers, tits and the rest of the chorus whooped and chattered around me. Masanabu Fukuoka talked of his "natural farming" not as an end point, an Eden, but as a "road back to nature"[15]: as I cycle out of the nursery, the solar lamps flickering on, peach flowers winking pink like the early tint of salmon sunset, it feels like we're on the road.

Fresh Pickings

March 5, 2012

This week, normal service is resumed: our box scheme members, stall supporters, and five catering partners will once again be enjoying Hawkwood salad.

There are many reasons why mixed salad leaves are our flagship product here. As a labour intensive, highly perishable and high value crop, they are the obvious thing to grow at a small community-supported market garden a mere cycle-trailer's ride from its marketplace. Ecologically speaking, they allow us to dispatch commercial quantities of one thing whilst side-stepping the dead end of monoculture: last year forty-three different species of plant passed through the mixing trough.

The mix evolves through the seasons, summer blend giving way to hardy leaves, enabling year-round supply. I say year round, but everything needs a break some of the time. Our corn salads and chicories get annual leave in January, when, for all anyone knows, they take long-haul cosmic flights to the Underworld and the Veneto. Then we commence picking before we leave Aquarius.

The best laid plans. This year, winter came hard and late, like Paul Scholes[16] on one of his bad days, nipping new growth. Frustrating, but the flip side has been seeing the eagerness with which a range of folk have been asking after it, and the cheer with which last week's first slim pickings of rocket were greeted.

Absence makes the heart fonder, I guess; or "you don't know what you got 'til it's gone", as Joni Mitchell chirped in that 1970 song of dawning environmental awareness[17]. I found myself gnawing ravenously at the "graded out" leaves as I sorted them last week, as if I too was starved, not only of the flavour and texture, but of some vital element held in these fresh raw greens.

More broadly, the hunger we are seeing in the cities for food with vitality, grown with integrity, hints at a yearning to retrieve what is gone or going: that natural fibre that threads us to our place in the world.

Yet always, after a going, a return. This week, our freshly-engraved bike trailers will be "Pedalling London grown food", satisfying at least some hungry people with one joy of a returning spring.

From Where Rhubarb Stems

March 13, 2012

This week we began picking the earliest of fruits in the Old Kitchen Garden, and in a soft-focus moment I remembered how, two years ago last month, a bunch of us set forth to navigate the Rhubarb Triangle as my birthday treat. This might seem a strange idea, but really, if you can't drag your mates off to a small village near Wakefield to spend an afternoon watching rhubarb grow in a shed on your birthday, then what, other than for being born, is the point of it in the first place?

It was a sight of eerie magnificence: as far as the eye could see, darkness, but for a few candles illuminating dense screaming crimson stalks stretching starwards with the simplest and surest faith in light.

A unique combination of environmental and social factors led to rhubarb production being concentrated in a frost pocket between Wakefield, Leeds and Bradford. Similar but different to those which made our Lea Valley the hotbed of glasshouse salads: for both, these factors have declined in importance, or disappeared, but a legacy continues.

For those in the Triangle, it's a living legacy to be proud of. Shortly after our visit (though, I regret to say, unconnected to it) Yorkshire Forced Rhubarb achieved European Protected Designation of Origin (PDO) status: only the second British fruit or veg to achieve it, after Jersey Royals; and putting it in the same league as Champagne wine, Parma ham and Kentish Ale. Yet while West Yorkshire may be the home of "champagne rhubarb", as this early crop is known, its origins are firmly rooted in the Thames Valley basin.

Into the nineteenth century, rhubarb was solely used as a medicinal herb, its root being an effective purgative. It's also an effective hair bleacher, and I guess I'm not the only fair-haired rhubarb grower to have been accused of resorting to this herbal dye. Fortunately, this smear didn't stick, as most people concede I must have some blonde genes, due to my undeniable gormlessness.

Gorm was also in short supply at the Chelsea Physic Garden in the winter of 1816, when some local tradesmen were repairing a wall. Job done, rubble and detritus were duly left on the Rheum rhabarbarum bed: that spring as ever, the gardeners were left to make good the builders' collateral damage. In so doing they found a collection of straining, bleached shoots desperately trying to push through the ruins. Natural curiosity being what it is, they sampled the freak plant growth, and found it to be much sweeter, more succulent and edible than the tough trunks they had hitherto known. Before long, rhubarb pies were being sold on London streets. By the end of the century, West Yorkshire folk had knocked up some forcing sheds and taken it to new scarlet heights[18].

"The best things in a garden happen by accident", says the almost infallible Monty Don. And like all accidents, they can come from some pretty surprising corners: for champagne rhubarb, their crowning achievement, northern horticulturalists have to thank not just a soft Londoner, but that most maligned of London characters, the cockney cowboy builder. Of Chelsea. If the Physic Garden had only taken the reasonable step of freezing their wall repairs budget until various brick taxes and imperial wars had settled down a bit, he might have been a Chelsea fan to boot.

Here at Hawkwood, we don't go to the stoic effort of digging up our "Timperly Early" and carting it off to be forced in a shed: instead, we blanche it in situ. We don't scatter London bricks, nor wool shoddy in the Pennine tradition: instead, the plastic fabric so beloved of the Lea Valley's remaining commercial growers. I doubt we'll ever get PDO status for our London Blanched Rhubarb. The smiling pink shank of this sweet and sour fruit of winter has to be reward enough.

Water of Life

March 27, 2012

It's rare to find myself on the same page as the capitalist media, but these days we're all agreed that this unseasonal dry spell is headline news.

A hosepipe ban begins in the south-east next week, whether or not the tradition of April Showers makes a welcome comeback. The ban won't affect commercial growers…yet. But Graham and Lizzie, our compañeros in the east, report that organic growers there are already scaling back this year's production plans. We'd be pondering a similar move had Huf, Norman and Pip not spent many hours last year at the gutter, looking at the stars, in order to divert the heavens that open up on the glasshouse roof into two 36,000 litre fonts.

Rainwater harvest, in these unsure times, is an obvious, but not necessarily simple, step for gardeners and growers. And water butts don't actually work unless it actually rains, regularly: I've yet to find a manufacturer offering any such guarantee.

Then there are the little leaks, previously unnoticed, that Huf, who "bottom lines" building and facilities, has been identifying. His idea of tapping the Victorian spring-fed well at the top of Spring Field has made a meteoric rise (or descent, depending on how you look at it) from Blue Sky Vision to possible inclusion in his next six-monthly work plan.

Ultimately, spring-fed wells don't actually work unless it actually rains, either. But what the current water crisis is doing is re-focusing our attention on how to make best use of the precious liquid that does enter, and exit, the site, something that is second nature to peasants in the dry lands.

Water is one of the many forces that flow through Hawkwood: with plants and panels, we're trying to better intercept and harness the solar power that pours down on us. And then there are people.

Human energy, and its wise use, was the theme of last Sunday's well-attended Open Day, with thoughtful yet active contributions from writer/ grower Rebecca Laughton, and our very own people person, Clare. Alumni from the most recent Permaculture Course returned to implement one of their design projects; whilst Pip and Naomi marked their last weekend here. They served as apprentices, before breaking into the ranks of BloGPeTHAs (Bloody Good People To Have Around). Now they embark on a voyage to join the dots of scattered land-based projects on this island and beyond.

This is how it flows here: people appear, for a day, a life, a while, a year, a spell: with questions, ideas, inspiration, hands, eyes and muscle. As project workers our job is to try to see that that energy is held, not leaked. This all seems to make sense. The question that still bugs me though is this: is raindancing a waste of energy?

Spring of Memories

March 4, 2013

Say what you like about them, but I wouldn't have got where I am today without a good food scandal every so often. The Tesco horsemeat saga[19] is merely the latest chapter: in recent memory, over the white noise of pesticide contamination, there's been salmonella, e-coli, foot and mouth, "mad cow", bird flu, genetic engineering. In the war of worlds, all battles lost by the military-industrial-agricultural world; all sparking minor flurries of interest in sustainable alternatives, some of which are sustained. The growth in organic food and farming – in localised food systems – over the last three decades, can be traced in some part to such publicised calamities.

These scandals serve as reminders, snoozed alarms, of what is going on relentlessly under our noses, even as attention drifts to the next news story. They are all legally born of the modern food system's complicated, heavy input and supply chain, tethered to the twisted logic of profit.

I think this is a time of reminders. The seed swap event at the Hornbeam Centre on Friday was a reminder of the eternal promise of seeds, and the power of cultural exchange and community: people power buzzing and swarming through the cracks in the edifices of corporate power, in the belly of London.

On the day the last of the dry asparagus stems was fed to the wood burner, we began mulching up the asparagus beds, remembering the sleek spears' sliding white to green, and their sublime spring succulence.

I'm remembering how the spring seed-sowing schedule is meant to go again; remembering to check on the plants again; rediscover them as they rediscover growth. They are remembering themselves. As we remember again, after The Long Trudge through the winter garden, how to handle the hoe and plug tray: we re-member ourselves of planet Earth.

The bird song, the freshest green, the chitting seed, the golden light. It all comes flooding back.

Something to Sprout About

March 17, 2013

"March comes in like a lion and goes out like a lamb", so they say. This year, the lion has been lying down with the lamb a lot. Over the glasshouse salads, the horticultural fleece has been going back and forth like a turnip hoer's elbow, as gladdening sun rapidly rotates to wild, wet and bitter cold. Yet the spring tide takes, irresistibly.

My biometric diary entries are heavily concentrated into March, April and May; the Firsty Times. All the great debuts occur here: the first blackthorn blossom; the first bee; the first hoverfly: through to the premier bluebells and mayflowers. All bring the news we all need to hear: we can start again.

In the garden, a series of firsts crests the ridge between bright and dark side. It is not uncommon to sow the first seeds (tomatoes, always tomatoes) indoors whilst the world outside freezes over. Even so, Wednesday was remarkable. Having issued notice to the winter compost heap residents that normal management operations would commence, we spent the day turning a good few tonnes of partially decomposed matter a few metres to the left. We moved a mountain. The day warmed a little, and the heat rose from the centre of the windrow. We were sweating and some of us stripped to T-shirts , as we dug on in the face of the blizzard.

Short sleeves in the snow. This is a tough month. A friend who worked through winter on farms in the Arctic Circle in Finland once told me that the real horrors – the suicides, domestic violence and narcotic oblivion – peak not in the depths of midwinter, when dark and ice have everyone in their absolute grip, but during the meltdown, just as the colour and warmth appear, but are not quite in grasp. Just a kiss away.

The labour, hope, movement for something better, which is in sight but still has to be worked at: this month deserves its own verb, Marching. As the rich ramp up their attacks on our lives, our communities, and our sweet earth, there is much to March about right now, in the streets…and in the fields and gardens.

In the latter, here at Hawkwood, there is glory. There are few more awesome sights in horticulture than the current two highlights; the pink stems of blanching rhubarb rising in the darkness of our Cockney Blanching Benders, fists of clenched golden leaves; and the almighty hatching of the tiny seed. We've taken to celebrating this time of germination by making spring our beansprout season. Beans, lentils, sometimes alfalfa, mustard, clover, are germinated indoors en masse, for inclusion in our weekly vegeboxes. Of course, we – and you – could be sprouting all year round, as many people do: but for us, sprouts' great niche is that they are a very quick-growing and nutritious something to help fill the looming Hungry Gap. In turn they help tune us in to the underlying energy of the moment, that of birth, renewal, awakening.

Later, we March out.

Searching for Some Spring

March 27, 2013

Across the land snow has driven the spring back in, making this the slowest start to a season since I began to record, if not since records began. Consequently, we've never been so prepared, with much of the winter work list fully ticked off, the ground still too wet to do the rest. Courtesy of Cathy and the City & Guilds Gardening class, we've even got round to getting the new tomato supports up, a good month — hopefully in more than one sense — before they will be pressed into action. You could have been fooled into thinking we were a highly organised operation, at least until we ran out of string, close to the raised beds' finish line.

I am slightly ashamed to declare that, in the life of this project, we've now got through nine kilometres of polypropylene twine: that's enough to tether the glasshouse to our distribution and outreach consulate, the Hornbeam Café in Walthamstow. Quite the purpose of doing such a thing is unclear, though, so maybe we've made the right move after all, in using the twine for plant supports.

Would that we could stitch a lifeline for other organic growers. The Hungry Gap arriving early after last year's famously poor harvests, the last thing needed was an extended hiatus before the spring crops mature. However much you squint at them, the short-range weather forecasts don't look too pretty: air temperatures of less than ten degrees do not a growing season make.

In the top corner of my little office pinboard is a quote from one of my organic growing gurus, Iain Tolhurst[20]: "If you worry about the weather, you are in the wrong job". I try to follow this teaching, and, like all religious followers, I am careful to find the loopholes in the text: there is nothing in Tolhurst's commandment that prohibits one from being grumpy about the weather, for a start.

With the light growing and the sap rising, it feels like spring's tightly coiled, ready to burst forth as soon as temperatures pick up. Stephen, Kate, Ian and I got the glory leg, finishing the heavy mulching of asparagus beds and paths, and right away I could hear the soft spears starting to stir. All we are all waiting for is for someone to bring us a bit of sunshine…

Perhaps it'll be the ten rescued hedgehogs Stephen will be bringing from South Essex Wildlife Centre. Or this year's influx of trainees. Usually, they start in April and have to hit the ground running: this year, Aimée, Jen, Olivia, Paul, Rob, Holly and Kristen will begin, next week, pretty much at the beginning. The seeds that have been sown sit, pent, on the glasshouse staging, the first stage of their brilliant journey. Unworried and unhurried.

Cress is More

March 18, 2014

Arguably our most valued crops here at Hawkwood are the winter salad leaves. They may lack the mass appeal of toms and strawbs, but they make up for this in longevity – spending up to twelve months in the ground; and in the dormant period their rare, dependable, fresh growth and emerald hue have us hunting and gathering them to the point of endangerment. But winter salads, like winter pansies, are in their pomp not in their appointed season, but in the sharp spring that bursts it.

The wild rocket, chicories and miners lettuce are all exuberant right now, especially under the glass, where their last mad surge of youth will soon outsprint us. The secateurs will give way to their flowers, the flowers in turn to the compost heap, then summer rolls in another rotation.

Of the more punchy ingredients, those cockle-warmers of the winter leaves, watercress has been especially good. Every year we grow a bit more of it, and every year we have no regrets. While OrganicLea was established to "sustainably rehabilitate the food growing heritage of the Lea Valley", a heritage we've explored in various publications and presentations, we've largely neglected the area's history of growing watercress, in favour of more cultivated plants of the garden. That is, until Hannah picked up the story in last week's Local Food News, our "in-house" news sheet.

A native of very wet ground, watercress would surely have been enjoyed by the first folk to hang around the Lea's marshes, and was likely harvested and managed in some way by the area's first farmers and gardeners, the Saxons in the sixth century. In the nineteenth century, Hackney became noted for its cultivation of said Rorippa nasturtium-aquatica, great stands of it in Morning Lane and Hackney Wick, fed by the flowing Hackney Brook as it bubbled into the Lea. But as Hackney became more definitely part of London, the water quality declined. A cholera outbreak in the early twentieth century was blamed on the cress, and that was curtains.

The spectre of polluted water, either by man or by sheep, in the case of the potentially fatal liver fluke, (rightly) continues to deter people from foraging the peppery creepers. But our watercress is safely reared on filtered rainwater, as are our beds of its rarer cousin, the Walthamstow Yellow Cress.

Hackney Brook is now many feet under the rumble of Morning Lane, though no doubt many gardeners in the area safely nurture a bunch or two; and perhaps those clumps of cress I spot thriving upriver, in the small weirs beside the Navigation's locks, are proud descendants of former aquatic gardens.

Curiously enough, watercress doesn't even need to be grown in water: it likes it damp, but can be happy in a soil bed, as in our glasshouse, as long as it's well irrigated. The habit of flooding watercress beds has, I believe, much to do with weed suppression, and with moderating cold temperatures, so making it such a reliable outdoor winter vegetable.

The winter, and its woeful water excess, is behind us now, leaving us washed up and warmed by the wealth of watercress and winter salad. In their current ascendancy, they are a reward for, and a lesson in, resilience: the resilience of all the gardeners who've been showing up here through the dark days. After troubled waters, the good times flow.

April

Peasants Revolt (2014)
OrganicLea joins the Landworkers' Alliance in a demonstration at the offices of the UK Government's Department for Environment Food And Rural Affairs (DEFRA)

Transglobal Underground

April 1, 2010

Last week we scrubbed up the warehouse into a "rustic" lecture theatre, to host a visit from Capital Growth groups and University College London's Development Planning Unit, who now run a module on Urban Agriculture (UA — being the vogue term for all forms of urban food growing).

Student presentations of various case studies reveal how UA, in the two-thirds world/ global south (or whichever moniker you choose to give to what we once called the underdeveloped nations) as well as here in Blighty, is increasingly being regarded not as an unsightly, embarrassing symptom of backwardness to be controlled, but rather a feature of the landscape to be accepted. Even, where food security issues are really starting to bite, to be encouraged.

The point was made that we would benefit from a kind of counter-colonial knowledge transfer of more developed UA models and techniques. It is in a similar spirit that permaculturalists and organic gardeners seek to reverse the dominant approach to the land — that of dominating it — by instead attempting to listen to nature and work with ecological processes and systems.

Our half-acre of glasshouse may be a fairly hard, synthetic micro-climate, but we have begun the work of inviting the outside environment back in, by sowing nectar-rich flowering strips, potting up nettle planters, and installing a promenade of ladybird and lacewing hotels, now touting for trade, all in a bid to strike a balance between aphid pests and their insect predators.

Amidst all the worries and denials about the environmental and social crises crashing around us, it is the realisation that we are, after all, capable of forming mutually beneficial relationships with each other, and with the natural world, that can cause you to sigh out loud. It's the same sigh I've let out this week on seeing the blackthorn blossom burst, and it will be repeated with the flowering of the peaches, apples, squashes...

Sighs, like yawns, have a certain infectious quality.

Magic and Lablab Beans

April 25, 2010

It never rains but it pours; it never shines but it scorches. For gardeners, perfect weather, like perfect soil, is something of a utopia, an ideal scenario by which to gauge the prevailing limitations. Perhaps we could be less phlegmatic and more content with what the skies send our way, but honestly, three weeks of drought: whatever happened to April Showers? They were a fine tradition, introduced to help young transplants put out healthy growth while their roots settle in. I don't understand why they've been scrapped this year: we've missed them.

That said, the dry heat provided the perfect backdrop for our "I Never Knew You Could Grow That Here!" skill share at Hawkwood last week. Forty people gathered, from London and beyond, to exchange information and experience on cultivating unusual subtropical vegetables in the UK. It was an inspiring day, with Robbie, a grower for OrganicLea's Cropshare scheme[21], stealing the show by turning up with his vigorous chow chow plant.

As a project aiming to reconnect people and food, growing and facilitating the growing of produce special to the different ethnic communities in east London has to be something of a priority. The annoying beauty of such produce is not merely that it is adapted to a different climatic zone, but that seed is not widely available commercially, rather passed on through the informal and gift economies of the various communities. After the workshop though, Clare decided to use the gardening connections she has built up with London Bangladeshis, and scored some kudu and lablab seed. On Thursday they were duly sowed, and we'll try to squeeze them into the glasshouse beds, by way of a trial, this year.

This entails a revision of the 2010 Planting Plan, something that is generally discouraged. The Rotations and Planting Plans have been agreed by consensus at a quorate OrganicLea Coop Hawkwood Project Meeting, after being handed up to me, etched on birch bark, by the goddess Hel, from the old well at the top of the site which drops into the underworld, at dusk on the winter solstice.

Our community gardening work attempts to thoughtfully and compassionately apply the natural and social sciences, but a bit of magic always helps. We'll certainly need it if we're going to be growing Asian vegetables in dark damp England.

Moon Flowers

April 5, 2011

This year, we've returned, cautiously,
to the practice of gardening by the moon.
This doesn't mean nocturnal weeding, though
we would benefit from a few more night patrols to catch slugs. Rather, it is the truly
ancient gardening practice of sowing, planting – even weeding and harvesting – to the
rhythm of the lunar cycle.

Lunar planting was largely sidelined by advances in soil science, though there
is clearly some scientific rationale, as well as a healthy handful of earth-based
spirituality, to it: after all, the waxing and waning of the moon affects tidal
movements, sap rise in trees, female menstruation and indeed human behaviour.
According to lunatics, you sow on the waxing moon as the rising waters encourage
germination, and plant out after the full moon, as the descending energy "pulls" roots
down.

All well and good, but whatever gardening you do, it's hard enough to stick to a
strict schedule, as the weather, garden developments, and other joys and chores of
life invariably combine to throw you off schedule much of the time. Which is why
I've previously tried and turned from the moonlight: just one more complication you
don't need. Then again, there's nothing like a challenge.

And so it was that on Thursday, as I was about to set off to celebrate spring in the
tradition of the Belgian cycling Classics, I had everyone rushing around planting
potatoes, shallots and salads that had been sitting around like lemons in the waning
window, watching the grapefruit moon extinguish.

Then next week, we'll be sowing three weeks' worth of seed – some 3,000 plugs.
Trying to keep with the lunar rhythm is reminding me a little of when I took my
two left feet to salsa classes. That said, and whether or not we detect any significant
improvements in plant growth as a result of our efforts, there is a satisfying sense of
reconnection and wholeness in this working with lunar, as well as solar, energy. An
occasional bit of mild panic is a small, perhaps a mandatory, price to pay for this.

Miners' Support

April 13, 2011

This year spring is on fast forward: it seems as though mayflowers, bluebells, daffs and anemone have all burst hotter on each others' heels than "usual", whatever that is. We are in the middle of a very dry spell that started well before the temperatures rose, and it's taken us by surprise here: the overhaul of our outdoor irrigation is at the all-important pipes-lying-outside-the-garage phase. But there have been some heroic trench-digging efforts from the likes of Vince, Sonny and Ed, and a new Age of Aquarius has dawned in Chingford, as the volunteer workforce cart water in old-school cans over to the thirsty young salads.

There is a rich mix of different nectars wafting around, but my particular favourite is the honeyed air put out by the miners lettuce, which embraces you when you open up the East Wing of the glasshouse of a morning.

Miners lettuce goes by various names, including: winter purslane – it is one of the wonder plants that "prefers" cool short days; spring beauty – an apt moniker, but one that seems to be applied to all members of its genus; claytonia – its botanical name, but I question the conceit of Mr. Clayton, and the rest of the colonial botanists, and their claims to have "discovered" native flora.

The common name I prefer at least tells the story of an honest people-plant relationship. Indigenous to the sparse mountain and coastal areas in the west of North America, when white folk headed wild west hoping to find fortune in the Californian Gold Rush in the 1850s, they found this trailing leaf was their main fresh vegetable, their main defence against scurvy and other deficiencies.

No doubt the Native Americans used and named the plant also, but that story has yet to reach these gardens, their numbers decimated by the Gold Rush wave of European disease and oppression. Back here in Boomtown, the miners' salvation is a big player in our mixed salads right now: it has a great succulent texture and a mild flavour which, like "real" lettuce, is vital in balancing the stronger tastes of mustard, rocket, coriander. Best of all for the salad grower at this time of year, as we try to check leaves turning into flowers, when in flower there is no adverse change in flavour or crunch: in fact, it's improved by the addition of a cluster of cute white blooms set strikingly in the centre of the leaf. And the morning golden rush: the best air freshener you can grow.

A Good Friday for Potatoes

April 9, 2012

On Thursday we were planting potatoes in the Entrance Field, when Clare pointed out it was the eve of the traditional potato planting day, Good Friday.

This custom is held to be as old as this side of the Atlantic's relationship with our favourite tuber. Its introduction in the sixteenth century was regarded with some suspicion, understandably for a relative of the known killer Deadly Nightshade. Irish Catholics were prepared to take the risk, though, covering themselves by sprinkling them with holy water and setting them out on the sacred day of the crucifixion.

A slightly later, more materialist explanation for the Easter rule is that the rural population of Britain, once they had been largely proletarianised, worked long and hard and were afforded little time off: the Holy Day was a rare holiday, and a moment seized to get the key bulk crop into the cottage gardens. A highly pragmatic act, and an assertion of their surviving spheres of independence; one carried forwards by urban working folk on their allotments ever since.

In this latitude, Easter is a pretty good time to trowel in chitted tatties, *more or less*: it rolls around the calendar, and Maundy Thursday can be up to six weeks later one year than another. This is because it is tied to the first full moon after the spring equinox. Timing planting out with the waning moon, as we attempt to here at Hawkwood (though allowing Chaos to have the final say) is a truly ancient technique, and one that fits perfectly with the Good Friday tradition.

The pagan festival of Eostre, on the equinox, which the like-sounding Christian festival hopped on to, celebrates renewal and germination: the sowing of seeds being a potent ritual, and eggs being the vital symbol. This has hatched the bizarre post-Christian convention of hunting chocolate eggs. As Mary, Giro and I lined the egg-like tubers in the trench and began concealing them with earth, yet another reason for linking spuds to the Last Supper appeared to materialise.

In gardening, as in the wider world, it is common for people to either reject old customs outright or indulge them unconditionally. But these extremes can miss the point somewhat: traditions can enrich our understanding once *layers* of meaning are let to form. And by realising the concurrent existence of a Now and a Then, we are able to see ourselves in a spiral that includes a Future.

By resurrecting old and heritage varieties, like this year's "Red Duke of York" and "Arran Victory" potatoes, at a community market garden in London's Lea Valley, we are not trying to hark back to an agrarian past, but attempting to connect things: modern technologies with ancient wisdom; supportive community with individual liberty; demonstrating other possible futures to the One Way Dead End dictated by the Biotechnological-industrial complex.

Forwards, not Back, to the Land! Pitchforks, Red Duke of Yorks, Fairtrade chocolate eggs in hand.

Asparagus Shoots and Slow Leaves

April 23, 2012

If nature is the best teacher, as a number of people whose views on things are generally worth listening to have suggested, then the garden is a decent comprehensive educational institution. One of the lessons I've learnt here is that learning itself is spiralling in form. So that, as the season calls, I find myself having to *re-learn* a technique or subject: the requirements of tomatoes say; or how to explain the importance of soil; or how to show someone you love them. Only not always from scratch.

To the less charitable this might smell a bit like an ecological excuse for my habit of repeating the same mistakes. A case in point might be my annual failure to consider the possibility of late frosts. The first of the asparagus will hopefully be the last of this year's victims, though Mary isn't too sure about the peach blossom. There is this human tendency, perhaps with an evolutionary function, to forget that cold weather exists when it's hot, and vice-versa. It's a tendency related to another of my recurring lessons, that of careless wishing.

In the dry warmth of March, I wished for rain, and a cool spell to slow plant growth: seedlings sown to be ready for the May plant stall had sped instead to their peak condition a month early. Sure enough, then came April, cold and damp. Sure, this has given us time to catch up, and banished watering worries, but be careful what you wish for: the winter salads are tiring but their spring sown successors remain sluggish, and stem rot is troubling the cucurbits. Now we want a bit of warmth back, and a dry spell so we can get out and hoe the fields effectively.

I suppose I need to cultivate a more patient, accepting, long-term attitude towards weather patterns. Maybe pin up the quote from a meteorological report I once heard on Radio 4: "if it's not raining where you are, it's about to. If it is, it will stop". I worry that climate change is making weather patterns even more unpredictable, but trust that with a continued faith in nature we'll get by.

A couple of weeks ago, Stefan remarked he could feel seven hundred asparagus plants pushing up against the topsoil. After three years of waiting, and a false start of frost damage, shooting spears were prized out for this Saturday's stalls. Some things are looking up.

Seems Like Years

April 10, 2013

"Little darling, it's been a long, cold, lonely winter, little darling, it seems like years since it's been clear." - The Beatles, Here Comes the Sun

Oli, our Building Development Worker, reckons it's been an eighteen-month winter: only a mild exaggeration. Nature the teacher, though, doesn't sit around feeling sorry for itself, but is patient and resourceful. Flower buds wait; seedlings go-slow; and, as the leaves do not register on the trees, the wood pigeons show surprising cunning in getting through the brassica netting, and diversify their diet to include our red clover and wild sorrel. It was beginning to look like we might have to follow suit, until this blessed week.

You can die of patience. The winter may have already dragged on too long for some gardeners' friends: many frogs, *newts* and hedgehogs will have slept too long to wake up; bees' supplies, too, run dry. Clare and Cathy have done what they can, and called an emergency wildlife gardening workshop at Hawkwood this Sunday, so local gardeners can take action to save some small souls as they rise exhausted. Maybe there *is* such a thing as society, after all.[22]

After the burst of shine at the weekend, some souls are starting to stir. Woodpeckers are rattling around the adjacent woodland; a few bumbles, butterflies and hoverflies have waved at us in the glasshouse. Yesterday the soil thermometer in the Entrance Field struck six degrees, heralding the start of the growing season.

Some three months after we first began mapping the site, in 2009, Sean cantered into the building with an amazed expression on his face, claiming to have stumbled upon "the magical realm". It turned out that this beautiful and mysteriously hidden hollow within the wildlife area had, in 1985, been dug out as a pond habitat for the endangered Great Crested Newt, with a small grant from the GLC and the blessing of their newt-loving leader, "Red Ken" Livingstone[23]. *Ken's Magical Realm,* as it has since became known, now homes the cob oven and fire pit; and is where Jonny has spent many a winter Wednesday magicking the most elaborate compost toilet.

The dramas of London's history echo even through its gardens. If you stroll down the hill from Ken's Magical Realm, you soon reach the newly-developed and freshly-named strip at the top of the West Bank Terrace. On Tuesday, we sowed clover and planted early potatoes at Thatcher's End. Tamped the dirt down.

Here comes the sun. *Doo doo doo doo.*

Laughing with the Land

April 30, 2013

I had an inkling this might happen.

    A *rush and a push* and a simultaneous explosion of blackthorn, peach, almond, gage, pear and apple. Never in a month of May Days have the bees got up to such a heady cocktail. Similarly the seedlings, sitting in a two-month sulk on the staging, lurch suddenly into becoming: all wanting to get outside *now*.

    Any minute now. Even in years of steadier defrosting, spring's *emergency* is a moment of nervous excitement, a brinking of stress and joy, for the gardener. Right now, this urban market gardener is chasing his tail and the only thing keeping things together is the amazing, steady work being done by the sowers, potters, cultivators, planters and grocers at Hawkwood. Somehow Hannah seems to find happy homes for not just the mixed salad and rhubarb, but also the endive, wild rocket and nettles, whatever fits and bursts they put on. Clare's maternity left a gaping hole in the crucial plant stall's portfolio, but Marlene has jumped into her veggie biker boots: *everything's gonna be alright*.

    Every week Jo & co play seedling Tetris, bravely attempting to wedge in trays and pots whose combined surface area exceeds that of the sought-after hot bench. Nights are still cold. Late frost hunches in the peripheral like a pickpocket. Plants are trollied out of the glasshouse, then back in a day later at the drop of a centigrade. Fleece still rolls back and forth across the beds. Late Friday evening, venturing out after the coop meeting to re-cover the chervil, asparagus shoots peeped at me over the soil surface parapet. More rummaging in the dusk for rolls of fleece. Sane people would be driven to distraction by all this to-ing and fro-ing. But you have to laugh; the sky was a picture.

    The deep winter mulching of the asparagus beds now seems a myth-like memory. At the time, feeding organic matter to beds showing no signs of life – death beds – seemed as much a faith-based ritual as a horticultural task. Of course, it's both. Miracles are a fact of life. Kneeling before the soil, the spears of *Gjimlin* (our Dutch cultivar) point straight up, directing your eyes to the patient sky.

    Early London asparagus on the stalls at the weekend, we had the last laugh. Out loud. With the land.

Letting Go
and Coming Back

April 1, 2014

"If you want to keep a plant, give it away!" Brian Holden rejoiced. We were in the Growing Communities' Springfield garden, about ten years ago, where for some time sithe, a kind of perennial scallion, had been cultivated in the allium round of the rotation. Brian had cultivated these from a few bulbs gifted to him a further few years previous by Sari, whose partner had cradled them over the ocean from his — and its — native Caribbean island of St.Kitts. We've picked up the story at the point where Sari enters the garden for the first time, and is thrilled to find a whole bed of sithe growing, having lost her original stock to some disease or pestilence.

My mind has returned to this moment and to Brian's profound utterance as, a year on from our planting out the wee rhizomes of the endangered Walthamstow Yellow Cress (see May 6, 2013), it has established well enough for us to propagate, and send it out into the wide world. As we reach the end of the Waltham Forest Cultivate Festival, there are now five guardians of this freak East End watercress, making its survival in this part of the world more certain, just as its original sole habitat on the Walthamstow reservoirs appears less so. Furthermore, I'm proud to report that Slow Food UK have ushered this shy leaf into the hallowed ranks of "Forgotten Foods", one of only nine vegetable foods to achieve the distinction. Forgotten but not gone, if our release strategy works.Such selling or gifting of plants and seeds, the letting go in order to keep, is a common practice that might be variously seen as generosity or enlightened self-interest. Or, to use the term popularised by Peter Kropotkin[24], "mutual aid". In his 1902 book of the same name, he presented extensive examples of how nature cooperates, within and across species, for shared benefit. Written shortly after Darwin, the concept provides a sane, rational and rich response to the tendency to reduce the notion of "survival of the fittest" to "every man for himself, and devil take the hindmost".Today, as in Kropotkin's time, this tendency has a powerful lobby.That's why the EU is seeking ways to outlaw the distribution of "unregistered" plants like sithe and the yellow cress[25].That's why genetic modification technology continues to be pushed, though it is failing in its own supposed objectives of reducing pesticide use and increasing yields; and it is driving small farmers into extinction, setting brother against sister and children against Mother Earth.

The garden in spring speaks of different possibilities, of working together for sensual and material abundance. In the glasshouse afternoon, the broad bean flowers emit a heaven-scent perfume better than any bottle.The bumblebees bumble about them, as bumblebees do, feeding themselves and performing the vital act of pollination. So we can eat, the beans can reproduce to fight another day, and, going underground, bacteria at the roots fix nitrogen for the following crop, whilst worm casts its dark magic. "The earth is made a common treasury for all", the Diggers proclaimed as they set about establishing their outlaw agricultural communities as the English Revolution reached its climax. They may have been naïve; still they weren't wrong.

Dust to Dust

April 9, 2014

"We are stardust. We are golden. And we've got to get ourselves. Back to the garden."
- Joni Mitchell, "Woodstock"

The wind blew in from Africa last week, just as the windflowers — as wood anenomes are prosaically known — arrived shyly in the wedge of ancient woodland here at Hawkwood. And the country was bathed in Saharan dust.

It wasn't the dust per se, but its mixing in with local petrochemical fumes, that led to the hazy days and air pollution warnings. And, while this may be a cry from London's latter day "pea soupers", it doesn't represent a sunny outlook for our atmosphere.

Yet there is something appealing about being able to place your hand on a fragment of iconic desert: a tangible, in your face reminder that we inhabit a joined-up planet; a reminder whistled, to the initiated, by the immigrant swallows and house martins that will not long be returning here on the crest of a current.

Prayers and praises to the wind. These weeks it blows hot then cold, wet and dry, changeably yet irresistibly carrying us into the growing season. Winter's perm-washed fields have been blow-dried, allowing us to set foot amongst them for essential weeding and sowings, and it seems likely we'll have some seed potato in the ground by the traditional Good Friday date, always a smashing feeling.

Spring salad planting is well underway, with sorrel, lettuce, rocket, beet leaf and wild rocket all hitting the ground running, and this season's Production team has been assembled: Vi, Gary, Aimée, Sofia, Rob Brandon and I, all of us backed up by the ranks of trainees, volunteers, learners and project workers that make this place grow. There are thrilling times ahead, though not without challenges: the mild winter's failure to knock pests back is already showing in the slug levels on the beds of emerging asparagus.

It's even dried out enough to dig the rotavator out. "The cut worm forgives the plough", said William Blake, and I still believe that the benefits, for soil and aerial biodiversity, of green manure leys outweighs the damage caused by having to turn them into the earth[26]. But any cultivation, especially one as aggressive as rotavating, loses soil carbon and nitrogen to the atmosphere. Up there, dust to dust, to a land who knows where? As I followed the machine up and back, pass after pass, I could only hope and trust that they carry with them specks of the Hawkwood spirit of solidarity, like a message in a bottle, like a glow in a smog.

And Another Spring
April 23, 2014

"Daniel and Morgan [two Forest of Dean free miners] reminded me of the hill farmers up on the moor where I live, clinging to an economically marginal way of life, because they experience physically its dignity and tradition. It is their heritage and their right, and they, perhaps unconsciously, create a deep and ancient freedom."
- Sara Maitland, Gossip From the Forest[27]

Blessed are the land workers, for they inherit the earth. And nothing but the earth. In the UK we scrape a living, or just drift into debt, pursuing a vocation which, though vital, is rendered barely viable by international capital. Those who turn their hands to the garden, the field and the forest, are fuelled only by the sense that this isn't the daftest thing we could be doing with our short spell on the planet; that, and the solidarity of those who share this sense.

This was brought home powerfully at the recent Landworkers' Alliance[28] Farm Walks in Devon. Chagfood CSA (Community Supported Agriculture) is a five-acre, horse-powered market garden on the edge of Dartmoor, while Shillingford Organics is a well-capitalised, forty-three-acre holding employing eight people, bathed in the English Riviera sun. Both balance the books thanks to the voluntary time put in by CSA members and WWOOFers respectively.

At OrganicLea, this gifting of time and effort is at the foundation and heart of what we do. The gardens at Hawkwood are largely managed by volunteers: their design and layout geared to this input. Thus, in town and country alike, the "action of a few thoughtful citizens"[29], on the site of production as well as in the market place, keeps organic vegetable growers growing, just as the mega-farms and super-markets rely on their subsidies and tax breaks from the powers that be.

This was one of the points made – alongside that time-honoured point that the point is to change it – on Thursday, as the same LWA marked International Peasants' Day (a day which itself marks the anniversary of the 1996 massacre of nineteen landless peasants in Brazil) with a demonstration outside the offices of the UK Government's Department for Environment, Food and Rural Affairs (DEFRA). As demonstrations go, it was very much a pagan-festival-meets-Saturday-fruit-and-veg-market-meets-larger-than-life-scarecrows-dressed-as-government-ministers-meets-international-peasant-chants-and-flags sort of affair. Between the lines of the songs and speeches, you could spot a certain swelling.

Periodically, Springs break out. In recent times, we've had the Arab Spring; before that the Prague Spring of 1968, back to the "Springtime of the Peoples" revolutions of 1848. Often, the liberating openings of a Spring dry; always a Fall. But to say, as I've heard it said, "it ends badly", is like drawing a full stop on the seasons: there is no ending, happy or bad: we have to keep going.

An English Spring is an outpouring to behold, worth all the withering, false starts and split ends that precede and follow it. At Hawkwood, the whole scene runs green, a naïve backdrop to the riot of colour, from the fruit blossom, ancient bluebells and ended kale; all giving their everything to the *love of worker bees*[30]. Asparagus and rhubarb grow before our eyes, drawn up by some higher calling. Here, and every elsewhere, we – land workers all – weed and mow, redefine the Old Ways; and reunite sweat and soil. That "deep and ancient freedom" rises again.

What's on today
11am: Potting on into the garden!
12.30pm: site tour
compost mixing
bean stringing
orchard clearing
*stake making
pea love
pea love
2–4pm
Strawbale building
3–5pm
Cropshare gathering

May

Local Headlines (2010)
The wheelbarrow-mounted notice board greets arrivals
to Hawkwood on work days and Open Days

When Plants Die

May 5, 2010

There is so much to sing about this week. The apple blossom is in full bloom on the ornamental Maluses here, and on the newly planted row of cordons. When I go, I want to be buried under an apple tree – not just so I can "live on" in the fruit (*"then we shall all have eaten thee"* as the Yorkshire national anthem has it[31]) but because the blossom is, I think, my favourite flower on this planet.

My thoughts aren't far from death right now: in spite of all the fresh new life emanating from the fields and glasshouses, the distressing fact is that the cucumbers are being killed left right and centre. It really is a crying shame: Louise, Lucille and Brian planted them beautifully by their climbing strings, after Sean had pulled the stops out to get the beds ready in time. There they stood resplendent for a week, before being steadily executed at soil level.

What to do about *problems*? You don't want to panic or jump to rash conclusions, but patient observation can allow things to escalate unchecked. In this case, within days half the crop was gone. However, we at least managed to establish, through early morning inspection, that it was woodlice. Yes, woodlice. So often I've leapt to their defence when other gardeners have unfairly scapegoated them for chewing plants: they tend to dine on dead matter and when they are seen in the vicinity of damage, they are almost always there as mere opportunists, taking a passing nibble on strawberry flesh slugs have bored in to, for instance, usually muttering "oh well, waste not want not" to each other.

And this is the thanks I get. A rare (but not unprecedented) case of them attacking unblemished, live, green material. I'm particularly upset as, as usual, amongst the cues I've sneaked in some melons. Melons are tricky blighters that I keep failing with, but I'm nothing if not determined, and this year was going to be our year, melons and me. Ah, the best laid plans…

It's not a good look, a grown man shaking his fists at two-centimetre-long crustaceans, but I'll rage and grieve this week and then, I hope, get over it. Tony Benn, not most famous for his gardening advice, orated that "there are no final victories and no final defeats" in doing so, explaining more about growing than any celebrity gardener (save perhaps Monty Don). We have back ups: there will be, albeit slightly later, a cucumber harvest at Hawkwood this year. And, after all, outside the apples are in blossom. No final victories, but right now we are winning. Happy May Days.

Lost to the Frost

May 18, 2010

Last week was the first time I felt confident enough to put the tender vegetables out to harden off, so Sod's Law dictated that we experienced an unexpected late frost: I can only apologise to everyone in the South East for bringing it upon us.

We lost 50 or so plants, which only hours before were in prime condition for the Saturday plant stall at the Hornbeam Centre. The only survivors were a few of the "Golden Bantam" sweetcorn, noteworthily enough. The tomatoes, squash, courgettes, French beans and nasturtiums all bit the ice.

I feel hurt, careless, stupid and guilty; but if I can persuade myself to adopt a more philosophical stance, I concede that this is the kind of error that many competent gardeners, growers, *humans,* commit. I live nestled in the warm bosom of the East End, five miles from the draughty edge of Essex that hosts Hawkwood Plant Nursery. Even if I'd realised just how chilly things were getting out in the sticks, by ten in the evening it's as much as I can do to send warm wishes to my shivering subtropicals, up the Lea Valley, against the north wind.

There are some advantages to the distance, mind: I'm still enjoying commuting against the flow, out of London in the morning, and that sense of *arrival* when I reach the gates of little Eden. At this point of the year, perhaps above any other, it really is a lush green paradise.

So what do growers do when the much longed for lush green growth and fragrant blossom burst forth upon the scene? Why! Dig, plough, mow and deflower of course. We've been making posies of strawberry flowers from the early and maincrop cultivars as we plant them out in the Entrance Field: they're one-year-old runners and the received wisdom is that you should encourage them to put energy into establishing good roots and leaves, giving them a stronger foundation from which to fruit and flower better over the next three years.

This is tough love indeed, and I can't quite bear to do it to the apple blossom, though the same principle applies to newly planted fruit trees. Instead, I've kept suggesting to Sean that we really should be cutting short the apples' floral display if we cared for their long-term fruitfulness, then wincing inside the glasshouse when he eventually took the hint.

There's a time to be soft and a time to be firm, though – as I found out to my cost – even the Met Office can't tell you exactly when those times are. Some gardeners interpret Jesus' cursing of the fig tree (Mark 11:12–14) as a reference to the need to restrict fig trees' roots in order to stimulate fruitfulness. Jesus also said, "He who brings forth the tomato plant into the northerly winds is surely a fool amongst men". Sometimes I'm glad the Book of Horticultural Revelations didn't make the final New Testament editor's cut.

The Growing Season!

May 30, 2010

There's no stopping us now: British summer, with its tempered light and heat, is bringing everything – especially seed sown veg plants and vitamin D-starved humans – out of their shells. Day by day the tomatoes and peppers are looking taller, stouter and tanning to a healthier deeper green hue. I had *Lycopersicon nervosa* (Tomato Worry – a common gardener's complaint) for a couple of weeks as greenfly caused significant leaf curl on them, especially the precious *Kondine Reds*. But Holly and I inspected on Thursday to find them virtually cleaned up: a combination of volunteer lacewing larvae and spiders, introduced ladybirds, soapy comfrey spray, and no shortage of emotional support from myself and Nicole, their Irrigator-In-Chief. Much has been written and researched about the beneficial effects of singing and talking to plants, but recently I've taken to yelling at them. Encouragement, that is, as if they were my football team or a Tour cyclist ascending the Alpe. Ultimately, I believe it's about giving attention and love, however you choose to do it.

The climbing French beans are now taller than me. Sure, when you're as vertically challenged as I am, you get used to having to look up to things, only not things that just a few weeks ago got lost in the creases of my palm. It's truly staggering, and makes you think perhaps *Jack and the Beanstalk* was an historical account after all.

The Entrance Field is taking shape. I'm really pleased with its appearance: it's starting to actually *look* like what you might get if you cross-pollinated the attention-to-detail of the gardener with the broad strokes of the commercial grower. A bit more colour required, but we've only got ourselves to blame for that, as we insist on ripping the flowers off the strawberries as soon as they emerge.

As yet, the pioneer strawberry and beetroot show no signs of interest from pests known or unknown. We're now planting leeks. Wireworm, which can be a problem for leeks (and indeed our potatoes) is resident in the field, as it often is in established grassland. But we thought we'd risk it on the basis that I laid out potato and carrot traps last year and didn't catch a single wireworm. True, anything that can turn itself into a click beetle is possibly clever enough to spot a trap when it sees one. But there's no way they'll have anticipated such vociferous support for the newly promoted green and white team when they're on The Field. Altogether now: *COME ON YOU LEE-EEKS!*

Despite No Rain

May 2, 2011

Everything is go. An exceptionally warm, dry April equals *action,* leaving little time for the reflection required for such musings as these. However, this weekend being May Day, there is an imperative to find some space for celebration.

The Entrance Field, a sad-looking, boggy and therefore neglected space for so many months, perks up and our attentions turn to it. Or vice versa: this is a virtuous circle to follow winter's downward spiral. (Note to self: more year-round interest might mean more regular attention and weeding, thus less resorting to the rotavator.) A lot of the root crops are in, and the strawberries are exuberant: they will bear splendid fruits come summer, if we get some rain.

The Old Kitchen Garden, after months of digging out bramble, couch and bindweed by hand, is now down to maincrop potatoes. The soil there is the best this site has to offer, a gift to us from past generations of Victorian gardeners, to whom a bounty of good honest spuds will be a fitting tribute. If we get some rain.

I'm pleased, almost to the point of smugness, that we've more or less dodged the spring salad gap: last week we began picking the spring sown lettuce, rocket and orache alongside their wintry counterparts, which have still yet to run to seed. So we can look forward to an uninterrupted flow of summer salads, though a little rain would help.

There's been a lot of watering going on out here lately, with lots of young plants – seedlings, annual veg, and freshly planted fruit trees and vines – to establish. Right now Brian is even out watering the compost heap. All the ingredients were thoroughly mixed a month ago, now Just Add Water. I have lost patience with the sky.

So far, the growing season is going quite well. A bit of rain and it'll be going swimmingly.

Saint Celery's

May 24, 2011

"Everything the power of the world does is done in a circle." - Black Elk

Going round in circles may be considered a futile activity in what is still the age of straight lines and boxes. Yet even now, some cycles of nature are widely observed and celebrated, notably in the way calendar dates mark the spinning of the years. For growers, every day is an anniversary, a festival, a saint's day. The seasonal tasks are ritualistically performed once again. And every plant has its time to shine. In the last few weeks we've had Strawberry Fayre, Plant Sale Eve, The Feast of Spring Garlic, Lettuce Day, and this week came Saint Celery's.

It's a controversial beatification for a plant commonly called the "devil's vegetable". Why this is the case we can but speculate: it's an ingredient strongly loved and hated in equal measure, like Marmite, or celery's close cousins fennel, coriander and caraway. In fact, all the aforementioned are delicious except for caraway, which is genuinely and profoundly disgusting, but some people just won't be told. All are in the carrot family (well, perhaps not Marmite), which also boasts notoriously poisonous specimens including hemlock water dropwort, a ringer for wild celery.

A further explanation is that, as foodstuffs go, celery is up there with peanuts in the allergen stakes, and for people with celery allergy, exposure can be fatal. However, I suspect a hint of Roman Catholic repression behind its demonisation, perhaps linked to the notion that celery is our only native aphrodisiac.

Is this notion, I wonder, in some way connected to the "Celery Song"[32], a sexually explicit chant sung by Chelsea fans in the 1980s, with accompanying brandished stalks, and which still occasionally breaks out in football grounds today? My feelings towards this particular anthem are ambivalent: it is invariably voiced in a sexist context, yet any hymn to a vegetable has to have something going for it.

There are areas of the Hawkwood site that have poor drainage and are prone to waterlogging; the bottom dip in the Entrance Field in particular. Celery being, in origin, a bog plant, it was the ideal candidate for this spot, and last year the vigour displayed by the "Tall Utah" cultivar there was extraordinary. However, the rotation, like all cycles, revolves. This week Naomi, Ed, Keith and I set to tickling the new seedlings out, half way up the hill, in bone-dry soil in the heat of this drought.

I can't be the first gardener to note that the act of kneeling to plant out is akin to praying in more than just its physical resemblance. A prayer for a new Eden. And on this Saint Celery's, a sacrifice to the rain clouds.

Out of the Shadows

May 8, 2012

After two years of active waiting, the asparagus crop is coming thick and fast. A fleeting, rare delicacy at the best of times, we're especially precious about these tender stems right now. The floods and cold spring have stilled the dawn of the British season: the national shortage seeing the cancellation of the annual asparagus festival. Our crown jewels have weathered frost and, so far, the flooded terrace, and now seem unstoppable: future fracases with horsetail and asparagus beetle hold no fear for them.

Marko and I were on the West Bank on Friday, prizing out the light-footed shafts from Subterranea for Saturday's stalls. Turning back at the end of a long row, I swear some of the shoots had grown in the time we were going over them. We could never calculate how many bunches in the bed: more would keep popping up while we were counting, like blessings.

The glasshouse has been an ark of a blessing the last forty days and nights. It's given us somewhere to stand to watch the ducks swim amongst the spinach, and enough of a microclimate to bring on the early lettuce, in marked contrast to the standstill outdoor specimens. While much of the ground has been too wet to walk or work on, we've been able to keep ourselves busy at the propagation stations, seeing to it that the seedlings are potted on and pepped up for the annual round of spring plant stalls.

This extra attention has ensured that the tender veg plants look remarkably good considering: more proof of the Chinese proverb "the best fertiliser is the gardener's shadow". And the early signs from the stalls are that, despite the Great Outdoors being greatly inclement right now, the call of nature is still drawing green fingered citizens out.

The success of plant stalls, like all stalls, is somewhat precarious. Even on the May Day weekend, plant nurseries' equivalent of Christmas time for sales, bad weather means bad takings. As community gardeners though, we believe that if someone can't afford to buy our organic tomatoes, we can at least offer them the means, and information, by which to grow their own organic tomatoes, for a smaller initial investment. And free conversations happen: little interactions amongst little people; lives change in little ways. Blink and you'll miss it.

Not much warmth, but the rain has eased, and we were finally able to set foot in the Old Kitchen Garden. Some of us were shocked at how well the broad beans – as well as the weeds – had come on: tall and flush with their two-tone flowers. It seems we're coming to that time of year, when things grow out from the gardeners' shadows, grow without you, without a care, without sunshine even, it appears.

Many Paths

May 15, 2012

"A path is little more than a habit that comes with a knowledge of a place. It is a sort of ritual of familiarity." -Wendell Berry, The Art Of The Commonplace

Any grower worth their earth salt should make regular inspections of their site: the land, soil, plants, animals, events. This may seem obvious, but in the golden heat of the gardener's day there is usually just enough time to fulfil the urgent tasks of the day, before the outside inside world beckons you back. Usually, once a week I manage to "get round", equipped with one main tool: eyes; and one main aim, renewing acquaintance with the whole, and the particular.

Sketched out, the main paths at Hawkwood resemble the veins of a leaf or the trickles of a watershed, enveloped by the peculiarly human artery of the boundary path. The scratched lines of access paths between raised beds fizz off the broad ways and into the dense neighbourhoods of cultivation. The wildlife corridor is like a deep lake; Ian's mown trails are the only bridges across it.

My weekly meander rarely takes an identical route, but follows seasonal patterns punctuated by topical highlights. In the winter I am more likely to beat the bounds, hunting for some sort of perspective that I know will lift once we arrive here, Maytime, when attention is drawn into the epicentres of emerging vegetable crops. In recent weeks, the bluebell, apple blossom, stitchwort and asparagus communities have put on their annual shows, well worth going out of your way for.

There was once a notion that we might designate an official "Sit Spot", a point on site allocated for communal observation and reflection. But no one space does equal justice to the multiplicity of meanings and values of a community market garden, plant nursery, training centre and nature reserve. I have my own favourite points, which, throughout the spinning year, give views to live for.

Poets' Corner is pressed into our highest, most south-easterly reach, under one of the site's majestic, tri-centurion oaks. It's named in honour of the nineteenth-century "peasant poet" John Clare, a fierce and beautiful critic of the Enclosures, who inhabited Epping Forest shortly before the episode of Hawk Wood's enclosure. It is likely that at some point during his stay, his own famous wonderings took him through our nook in the forest. Nowadays, from the oakshade you look out over the Lea Valley reservoirs, the glasshouse, and the curving lines of Entrance Field vegetables. Amongst them, you'll likely see a crow pecking for grubs. Were she to fly due north from you, she'd arrive where three paths meet, at the head of the Old Kitchen Garden.

Here is as close as you get to a panorama at Hawkwood. The wedge of ancient woodland drops off to the Spring Field meadow, then behind the next tree line the high rise blocks of Edmonton remind you where you are, London Town. To your right right now if there's a gentle breeze you'll note the rippling silver of the bean plants, catch their soft sweet pea scent. On Friday, as the rain let up to finally allow the soil to drain, we were able at last to work the broad beans, relieving them of the tall, rain-swollen goosegrass that was beginning to suffocate them.

We set amongst them, myopically freeing one stem after another, stopping only to take in the markings of a ladybird or the just visible apparition of minute bean pods forming. After so many walkabouts where I could only look over the beans in their multitude, with admiration and mounting concern, this felt like I'd walked home.

Poetry and Flour

May 28, 2012

At last the sun has burned through the rainsmoke, and here at Hawkwood last week people were wearing bright hats and smiles as they set about preparing the ground for the sweetcorn blocs out on the Entrance Field.

When thin green seedlings, it's more easy to grasp the surprising fact that corn belongs to the grass family, *Poaceae*. This is a Greek word, though surprisingly unrelated to another Greek word, *poesis*, to create. Yet the Indigenous Mexicans call themselves "the people of the maize", as if the plant created them. A *poetic* notion maybe, but haven't those other grasses – sorghum, millet, rice, oats, barley, wheat – made our culture and society, for better and worse?

Into the beds will go "Golden Bantam", one of the few commercially available open-pollinated (i.e. not F1 Hybrid) cultivars, and "Bloody Butcher", a non-commercially available, heritage variety, whose kernel colour is, as the name implies, every bit as bloody as the mission to civilise the New World is.

At the weekend, some of us headed out to Rothamsted, to a very different *Poaceae* patch. There, more than 400 growers, bakers and families from across England, Ireland, Scotland, Wales, France and Belgium marched against the return of open air trials of genetically modified (GM) wheat.

It's in the make-up of well-intentioned and well-bankrolled scientists to narrow the debate about genetic engineering to small details, so that you can't see the maze for the maize. Standing back allows us to see the bigger design, and ask more fundamental questions. Like, should we work with nature, or against it? Should life-forms be patented, commodified, privatised? Who should be more in control of food production: the corporation, or the truly creative people, the producers?

With our hands, we create; with our hands, we destroy. We plant, and we weed. There is a time to give flowers; and, as the renewed GM campaign so rightly points out, a time to *take the flour back*.[33]

On the Yellow-Cress Road

May 6, 2013

"The best things in any garden happen by accident."- Monty Don[34]

Our loyal box scheme members and market stall supporters will this week receive something very special in their salad bags: leaves of the Walthamstow Yellow Cress.

I began trudging the Yellow-Cress Road at the start of this millennium. I had moved to Walthamstow, in the London Borough of Waltham Forest. The council there had marked the centenary of the death of its most celebrated son, William Morris, in 1996, and by the time I arrived they had still, quite understandably, not managed to bring themselves to take down the party decorations. His portrait was pinned to many of the town's streetlights, like a Robert Mugabe or a Chairman Mao: for a moment I thought I might have stepped into some Arts & Crafts socialist utopia.

It didn't take long to be disillusioned, yet here I stayed. I had come to pursue the vision of OrganicLea: "to sustainably rehabilitate the food growing heritage of the Lea Valley", a vision to which, of all the landowners in the Lea Valley, only the aforementioned council had offered any practical assistance.

Around this time I was reading the latest book by Richard Mabey. The botanist and writer, perhaps still most famous for his seminal foraging manual *Food For Free*, had published his epic guide to UK plants and their social relevance, *Flora Britannica*. Much of the book concerned plant lore from exotic rural locations I could only dream of, but one small entry leapt out at me:

"An up-and-coming cousin of watercress is Walthamstow Yellow Cress, Rorripa x armoracioides, a speciality of the damp wasteland round Walthamstow Reservoirs in London".

Magic. Our little unassuming corner of east London had, hidden away, its very own variety of watercress. Surely this deserved further investigation; bringing to light; celebration. Trouble was, the cress really was hidden away. The reservoirs were, or so I thought, the preserve of a few anglers, and even if I could sneak in under the pretence of fishing, I would end up scouring vast bodies of water for a particular, undescribed form of watercress: needles and haystacks came to mind, only with a higher likelihood of getting my feet soaked. The trail went cold for a decade or so.

Despite the hype I, like many people in the Lea Valley, found nothing to thank the 2012 Olympic Games for: save the one, following, thing. Inevitably, a small portion of all the money being sloshed around was grasped to fund some interesting fringe cultural activities: one was a botanical boat cruise of the Lower Lea, narrated by none other than Mr. Mabey. Just like the sporting spectacle, tickets for this were hard to come by, but at least one deserving local got hold of one: my friend Nicole, a founding mother of OrganicLea.

Agent Nicole was duly dispatched to make enquiries as to the whereabouts of the now grail-like wildflower, but the mission was an anti-climax. Mabey had no recollection of the Walthamstow. He stated, in his defence, that it had been a long time since he had researched the book. A fair point: but the fact that the yellow cress had become extinct even in the mind of edible weeds' most public champion made my chances of finding the plant, and perhaps the plant's chances of protection, that bit slimmer.

Suddenly and unexpectedly, a serendipitous meeting shortly afterwards turned things around, for good. Anaelle, one of OrganicLea's garden outreach workers, had been training gardeners at the wonderful "Living Under One Sun" community garden in Tottenham. For their end-of-course summer trip they came to Hawkwood. Amongst their number was a botanist called Brian Wurzell, who was fascinated by our plant life: not so much, I have to admit, by our resplendent vegetable cultivars as our rare forms of fungal disease: but that's another story. Knowing, by reputation, that Brian had carried out ecological studies in the region for a number of years, I thought to ask him if, by chance, he had ever heard tell of the mythical yellow cress. "Yes", he replied without hesitation, "I discovered it!" Cue bright light and choirs of angels.

Here, in the words of a subsequent e-mail from Brian, are the facts: "I originally found [it] close to the Lockwood Reservoir in 1971, was totally baffled and eventually, in 1974, was directed by the BSBI[35] to send a specimen to Dr. Bengt Jonsell at Uppsala University, Sweden. He replied straightaway to give me its name, Rorippa x armoracioides, and its parental ancestors, R. austriaca and R. sylvestris. It was already known in Scandinavia but this was the first record for GB. The English name which commemorates its original site is again given in Clive Stace's *New Flora*" (which is kind of the bible for serious botanists).

Immediately Brian seized on my interest in the plant, as he was concerned that it was seriously threatened in its current location. Thus it was on a bright Guy Fawkes Day 02012 that he took me to Walthamstow reservoirs, "our Lake District" as he calls it, and showed me the original site of discovery and, low and behold, more precious than gold, the flower of Waltham Forest.

He had eventually found the plant in two other London locations, both of which had since been built on, and the original Lockwood colony has been reduced – first by the building of a ring main over half of its extent, and now by the rapid encroachment of Himalayan giant blackberry into the remainder. Having sought the permission of the Fishery, I dug up a number of rhizomes already struggling in the shade of the bramble, and set off to Hawkwood to pot them up immediately.

Here, they were brought on in trays, left outside through a harsh Scandinavian-style winter, then brought back in again to get it flushing early. The yellow cress was, alongside lettuce "Cerbiatta", our first transplant of the year to go out, planted by myself, Aimée and Jem one fine April day in spring's youth.

Although in the watercress genus, the yellow cress neither shares a close appearance, nor the habitats, of the former. It grows in rough grassland, and looks not unlike the oriental salad Mizuna, with its light green colour, serrated leaves and slight hairiness. Though Brian himself had never tasted the plant, we assumed that any relative of watercress must have salading potential.

The yellow cress has a mild, mustard flavour, that might be unpalatable if you were faced with a huge plateful of it, but adds a fine piquancy to a bowl of mixed salad leaves. I've always felt that a mixed salad was a preferable ideal of a multi-cultural society than a melting pot: that different additions can complement, and temper, each other, creating something greater than the sum of its parts, rather than reducing them to a common denominator. In its finer moments, Walthamstow, a town of great social diversity with no one dominant group, achieves this.

At the risk of taking such plant-people analogies a little far – which is not something that has ever worried me before, mind – I love the yellow cress because it is a true Walthamstownian. Which is to say, like all East Enders, it is an immigrant to these parts. Brian posits that it most likely arrived here, as a piece of vegetative material or seed (though most of the cress' seed is sterile), on the feet of a bird migrating from Northern Scandinavia. The cress might theoretically have settled anywhere in this green and pleasant land, or beyond, yet it found its niche here, in this rough patch of city earth, after the splendour of the fjords. Like I did, hailing from the rolling fields of Hertfordshire; or our Tuesday volunteer Nava, transplanted from the farmlands of Sri Lanka: we all find something of beauty, something worth living and fighting for, in this Dirty Old Town, though we may not have ended up here wholly by choice.

We hope you enjoy the taste of the Walthamstow Yellow Cress, and that you may become as glad of this plant as we are: glad of our communities, our wild and cultivated places, our capacity to rescue one another, and our ability to surprise one another, surprise ourselves.

Into the Blue

May 20, 2013

Super busy. The myopic May focus on urgent sowing, cultivation and planting requirements often shields you from the garden's unravelling beauty surrounding you. But you can always rely on something from sideways knocking you sideways, out of the blue.

A lot comes out of the blue in late spring. It makes you wonder if the blue is a little congested the rest of the time. Unsurprisingly perhaps, it's our fallows at Hawkwood that often surprise me most. In the green manure beds under glass, phacelia and buckwheat are in head-turning bloom right now. The latter joined flowers of chervil, mustard, watercress, rocket and calendula in this week's edible bouquets crafted by Pretty Delicious. These went with three hundred potted plants, including wild rocket, cornflower, lemon balm, mint, oregano, alfalfa, nasturtium and viola, which we raised at shotgun speed, to adorn the tables at Deesha and Vishal's wedding on Saturday. Chives and borage never looked so happy as when I pushed them down the glasshouse aisle in the Danish trolley. Just the right amount of better and worse weather.

White petals of bird cherry and apple are starting to confetti the soils now. Four beds of squash are planted up. The plants were willing but the air a little bleak. They need a bit more warmth to grow or they may perish: every burst of sunshine is to be greeted now, and on Wednesday we did our version of a sundance, planting out sunflowers amidst the chicory on the Entrance Field. Sunflowers famously follow the sun as it arcs through the sky, so perhaps there is a tiny reverse attraction. It's a long shot, but so is the sowing of tomato seed in freezing February.

Under the protection of the glass, the tomatoes are now shrub size, in need of their first sideshooting. Hannnah says tomato pinching season is wedding season: on countless occasions she's been sitting at the banquet and asked to explain her green-stained hands. I tell volunteers that the quickest way to acquire green fingers is to pinch out tomatoes. I think it's true.

And on Friday the first of the spring-sown salads made it into the mix. It's a lettuce, "Sadawi", a deep red loose-leaf type. It is buttery and full flavoured with no bitterness. After a winter without, I didn't realise how much I missed lettuce, how good it can taste.

Soon we will be awash with the stuff, and we will start taking it for granted. Something else will jump out from the blue to be flavour or colour of the month. The cuckoo is back, announcing that the season is fully under way, and young, stretched before us, the possibilities all but endless and only vanishing where the land meets the blue.

Walking Talking Plants

May 27, 2013

Our plant sales season comes to a close, as nature's rhythm subtly breaks from birth/ germination to growth/ planting out. There's not much we do all year round, only drink tea, ponder the weather and mixed salad leaves. The latter remain constant, though constantly changing. Not for us the monotony of year-round tomatoes. Variety is the spice, after all; chilli varieties, the spici*est*.

For the plants season though, which basically runs between the two May Bank Holidays, I'm proud that we continue to operate as a plant nursery. In doing so, we honour our forebears, the council gardeners at Hawkwood Central, as it then was, in the days when local councils had the power and pride to be this country's chief employers of horticulturalists.

Adopting the fine glass roofed infrastructure from this era, we feel the sense of responsibility to make the facility a resource for the burgeoning urban food growing scene of which we are a part. In particular, many gardeners in our crowded town have little access to protected places to bring on tender vegetables. Our intensive care unit, as I call the glasshouse staging, is on hand.

Then, every so often, our plantlets find themselves in some unexpected and wonderful London scenes. They've been handed out as free gifts on the streets of Brixton, for example, and supplied a summer holiday's worth of activity for Somerford Grove Kids' Gardening Club. Last Thursday, Brian and I drove (actually, Brian did the driving as I can't, though I did help by nodding knowingly whilst looking at the map on more than one occasion) over a thousand young vegetables down to the South Bank. Here, Wayward Plants are planting up the Queens Walk Window Gardens for this summer's "Festival of Neighbourhood". It's estimated that some eight million visitors will cast their eyes over our "Cherokee Trail of Tears" French beans; thousands will catch our "Carter's Golden Sunrise" tomato glowing at Waterloo Sunset. No pressure then.

Jarred Henderson of Wayward Plants came to us because he wanted their contribution to an event purporting to be about London communities to be grown by a London community organisation. This might seem obvious, but people with that sort of clear vision and courage of their convictions are thin on the ground. Likewise, the chefs we work with – those at Friends House, Manna, Nice Green Van and Table 7 the most longstanding of them – have sought out, and risen to the challenges, of our local, seasonal produce, where others might be happier to just talk the talk.

Walking the talk: at our Open Day on Sunday, Iain Tolhurst gave a *talk* and joined the site *walk*. He is one of the "pioneers", who read *Silent Spring* in the early 1970s and decided that heading to the countryside to establish an organic farm was one vital way to confront the horrors of industrial agriculture, and present an alternative. Thirty-seven years later, his "stockfree" system, fully developed at Hardwick near Reading, has informed and inspired the next generation of organic growers, some of whom are taking the fight back into the cities. Maybe see you there.

Spinach, Cartoons and the Flower Moon

May 5, 2014

Next week's full moon is, in the Native American lunar lexicon, the "Planting Moon" or "Flower Moon", denoting the time when, for overwintered plants, there is a seismic shift in balance: from spring's leafy, lush energy rush to May Day's more power to the flower. Indeed, it's cheers and cheerio to the last of the bolting winter salads, and, out in the Entrance Field, to the spinach.

Adam lobbied hard last year for more spinach to fill the Hungry Gap, so we've held back on the following beetroot crop; we are still picking hard for the box scheme, and it's still giving, generous plant that it is. Brandon, the newest and youngest member of the production team, has probably picked more of the stuff in the last month than he's ever eaten. But everything has its limits: the stems are lengthening with the days, so flowers will surely follow: I think this full moon may ceremoniously mark their total eclipse on the Produce List.

The town of Alma, Arkansas, self-declared "Spinach Capital of the World", has at its centre a bronze statue of Popeye the Sailor Man, in honour of his unparalleled contribution to the growth in popularity of this green goosefoot. And rightly so: there can be few characters, fictional or otherwise, who have so raised the profile of any particular vegetable to such an extent. Jack sparked considerable curiosity in climbing beans; Bugs Bunny unashamedly and unstintingly product-placed carrots; Bodger and Badger waxed lyrical of their love for mashed potatoes. Charlie Brown and friends pushed pumpkins at Hallowe'en; sports scientists' latest performance enhancing's dug beetroot; and recent advice from nutritionists has seen kale sales through the roof in the last year. But since the 1930s, we've all grown up knowing that spinach gives good guys the strength to overcome brute evil, with Olive Oil at the side.

It's no mere comic fable either: the leaves are phenomenally rich in potassium, calcium, iron, sodium, carotene and folic acid, so can certainly "contribute to physical health and fitness as part of a balanced diet", as a modern remake of a Popeye cartoon might be required to disclaim. For a naval officer, spinach in the tinned form makes an ideal nutrient source for long voyages with limited cooking fuel. Note also how sea beet, the mother of our perpetual spinach, grows most profusely in coastal areas, including on this island, where its wind-resistant glossy shields throw themselves gleefully around in the strong salty winds. Here, it has surely been utilised as a vegetable since the dawn of the human age, and certainly way before cultivated forms emerged in the first century AD.

Yet here and beyond lies confusion. The hardy, reliable perpetual spinach, or leaf beet, favoured by so many gardeners and growers for its ease of cultivation, is in the same family, but a totally different storm-kettle of fish to the mild, tender, baby leaves of "true spinach", Spinacea oleracea, so beloved of chefs. The latter is a fussy plant, prone to bolting without regard to what the moon might be, and yellowing without regard to Adam's box scheme requirements.

On the other hand, true spinach is soft, buttery, sweet and delicious raw, where leaf beet is a tad metallic and coarse, and certainly, in my view, better off cooked. So the debate rages back and forth between the cultivators and the cooks as to which is the "best" type to grow. In recent years, us organic growers have probably not helped matters by marketing both ubiquitously as "spinach", causing crushed expectations in kitchens around the country. In mitigation, this is a time-honoured, cross-cultural conflation. I've talked to Bengali allotment gardeners to whom "saag" is spinach or, when it comes to it, any old green leaf that cooks down quickly. Carribeans sometimes toss the term "callaloo" about just as freely, bewildering those of us who have learnt from our "World In Your Kitchen" cookbooks that the term refers simply to leaf amaranth. And us Limeys are on no moral cliff-top here: for years we've lumped a cornucopia of wonderfully distinct edible flora into the sloppy serving of "greens".

Perhaps then, we should not worry unduly about getting ourselves into a spinach spin, and make a virtue of the ambiguity. After all, both versions have a similar vitamin and mineral make-up, and I'll bet Popeye would chuck either down his throat when called once again to leap to the defence of Olive Oil. Like yer mum said, just eat your greens. True story.

Learning from Nature

May 30, 2014

Very few gardeners are not also garden visitors; and, to a point, the converse is also true. In this way gardening, more than, say, Formula One racing or the opera, offers numerous fertile pathways between democratic participation and the Spectacle. As with any broadly creative pursuit, garden creators can be too immersed in the subject to see it in its entirety, in the moment, as the outside observer can. For the latter, the land can be still, a snap shot, whereas for the site worker it is all process, never a finished piece. I enjoy regular recreational walks round our little cultivated clearing in the Forest, but don't always capture an unobstructed view of the wood for the trees, the garden for the weeds, the field for its soil needs.

I make it my business, then, not to mind my own business now and then throughout the season: visits to farms and gardens form part of my work plan. This year, Shillingford and Chagford in Devon; in London Town, Sutton Community Farm, St. Matts and Kynaston Patchwork sites, have had to suffer pokes from my big nose. It's not just the odd new plant or new trick I'm sniffing around for, but to experience a growing space as it is, naked of to-do lists.

This is not to say satori[36] moments don't happen to me or the other gardeners here at Hawkwood; only, the stars have to be aligned and the plant combinations have to reach their moment of supreme poise. A moment in a million, just a few times a season. After a few years on the land though, you start to sense it coming. And any minute now, I know I'm going to blunder into the glasshouse and be stopped in my tracks by a picture of perfection.

Here, the flowering strips, and the cordon tomatoes intercropped with mixed lettuces and herbs, are on the verge of greatness. It's noteworthy that these early beds were sown and planted by the Level 2 Gardening course, a fact I take great pleasure from. When I formally studied horticulture, much of my class' practical assignments were rotavated back into the ground the following day, while others were tucked out of sight of the public garden, receiving little ongoing maintenance between sessions. We learnt, the hard way, the value of regular irrigation, and that plant pests didn't actually take Easter breaks.

At Hawkwood, we wanted to do things a little differently, to fully integrate course participants into the garden work schedule. Sure it takes some coordination, but we wanted the garden and the learners to get the most out of each other. And, after many terms of extra-curricular work by Clare, our Training & Outreach Worker, I think we have symbiosis. Last year, fifty-six people completed the Level One Practical Gardening Skills course here, graduating back to the land in myriad ways while making a real contribution to the local food economy through their structured practical sessions.

In nature news, we appear to have pied wagtails nesting in the glasshouse alongside the two magpies, who I'm still not sure are one hundred per cent welcome. The rare

Nathusius' pipistrelle bat is one of five species recently monitored flashing across our fields after sunset, and last week I opened the warehouse door to find myself face to beak with a tiny blue tit, nesting material still wrapped around its tiny feet. This year, the tits nested in the tool shed: a source of intense squeaks and wonder. Then, after another fledgling was spotted in the glasshouse, peering in on the coursework, on Friday, it all went quiet.

End of May, 2014. Learning to fly.

June

Pure Leaf

June 9, 2010

We've been producing salad leaves at Hawkwood for over a year now, in containers, but now the West Bank, our "Salad Central", is starting to give us salads grown *in the ground*.

It's one type of leaf per bed, so the range of tastes and colour is at present quite narrow, but once we've got one terrace of thirty-four beds dug and planted up, the diversity of leaf will become quite impressive. At Growing Communities[37] the salad bags boast over forty species – and some sixty cultivars – over the year, plus a fine range of edible flowers – and I think that represents something of a panacea that we would like to approach.

As well as supplying our own market stall and box scheme, we've now got an outlet in the "local village" of North Chingford. The Deli Station is this week testing our salad bags out on its customers, as well as supplying Table 7 restaurant. Jo from the Deli was here on Friday and perhaps was struck, as I have been, by just how "clean" all the leaves are: the plants are not yet showing one leaf that needs "grading out" due to pest, disease, old age or boredom.

To be honest it's almost *too* perfect, but we should revel in it while we can. I know only too well that sustained cultivation in one place can have the benefit of improving soil structure, but can also create great conditions for pest and disease build-up. It's a reminder of the importance of rotating, moving around, and observing breaks. For me, that means strolling around the whole site once a week with a cup of tea. This month the tea rotation shifts from nettle to elderflower. Tastes perfect.

The Joys of Weeding

June 20, 2010

On Thursday Sarah and I did a spot of weeding in the Entrance Field. I love weeding. It's like the gardening equivalent of sewing your stitch in time, or clearing your e-mail inbox, and I gain the same elusive sense of fundamental satisfaction from performing it. It seems to make the difference between living and surviving.

I especially love hoeing: it's primary care as opposed to firefighting, and the simple grace of the hoeing action seems to embody that fact. Walthamstownians of old loved hoes too: OrganicLea's office, distribution and outreach "hub" is situated on 458 *Hoe Street*, a thin ridge of a path that they thus read as the gardening work of some giant or goddess.

We have a fine selection of hoes: "English" draw hoes; "Dutch" push hoes; 2-for-1 push-pull hoes; oscillating hoes; onion hoes; wheel hoes and even the paradoxically-titled digging hoe. All have spent the spring and early summer hung up in the tool shed like forlorn pub decorations, while we plant out everything at precise hoe-width spacings in the – at times optimistic – belief that one day we might find time to go back and administer after care. Only this week can we begin to feel vindicated.

How fitting that the hoes are drawn in time for the summer solstice, that time of perfect balance and poise, and the occasion of our evening of celebration here at Hawkwood. We're throwing a party for all our workers, supporters and associates, with horticultural games, solar cooking demonstrations, a feast, elderflower champagne, and a traditional barn dance in our straw-rammed warehouse. I think for the first time I am really going to appreciate what it means to have a proper *hoe-down*.

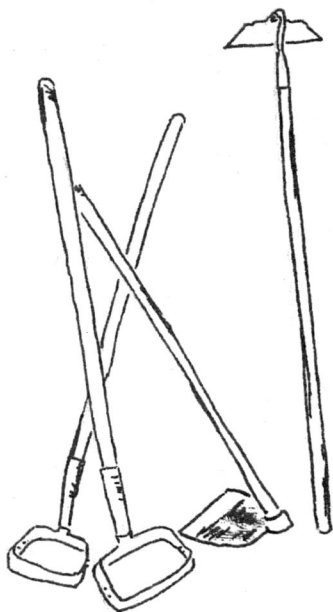

By any Beans Necessary

June 24, 2010

We will start picking beans tomorrow. The climbing French beans in the glasshouse have wowed us all with their mauve flowers and their stature, and now their speckled fruit are pencil-thick and ripe for the eating. They should be followed stringlessly by the dwarf French beans in the Entrance Field come August, so we'll be beanfeasting throughout the summer, then stop and leave the remainder to dry *on the vine*, to be used as a high protein pulse throughout the next year. All peas and beans can be grown on to pulses. We don't tend to do it so much in this country – either in the garden or commercially – but I believe in a more sensible, sensitive world we would do.

The plan was to concentrate on the flat-podded "Helda" beans under glass, but in the event I managed to rot them by over-zealous soaking of the seed, so "Cherokee Trail of Tears" became our main cultivar. It is fast growing, fast maturing, pretty and productive, and has its own story to tell.

In 1829, gold was found in Georgia, Southwest USA, under Cherokee homeland. This prompted the Georgia gold rush, and moves by the government to "relocate" the Cherokee people to reservations in the "Indian Territory" (now Oklahoma). An army of 7,000 rounded up 13,000 Cherokees into concentration camps, destroyed their homes, then forced them to march the 1,000 miles through the freezing winter of 1838.

By the time they arrived, 4,000 of their number had died of disease, starvation, cold and the occasional murder as they passed inhospitable settlements. The black seeded bean was carried with them on this *trail of tears*, and was planted as the bitter winter thawed to spring on the reservation. It is still grown by Cherokees, and other gardeners interested in "heritage" seeds, to this day.

I see the beanstalks growing in the glasshouse, tiny pods pushing out from the shrivelling violet blooms, and see them as living sculptures, symbolising the cruel destructive side to White/ Western/ Judeao-Christian culture; and also the spirit of hope and renewal represented by nature and nature-worshipping peoples.

Magic Beans
and Tragic Beans

June 27, 2011

For all the exotic pungency of roses or jasmine, it's the subtle, elusive nature of the scents of plants like gorse and peas that make them more bewitching. And a field of beans is to the nose what a woodland floor of bluebells is to the eyes: a glowing, cumulative aroma that wafts immeasurably in the wind.

Our row of broad beans issued a mere suggestion of this when in flower, and now the plants are in gloriously bulbous pod. They conjure more besides: the humble allotment gardener's broad bean, *Vicia faba*, when dried yields the Classical "fava" pulse so vital to Egyptian, Greek and Roman diets. To this day fava beans are poplar in the Middle East, in, amongst other dishes, authentic falafel, but are largely confined to animal food on these shores. This winter we plan to make the Kitchen Garden a small "beanfield" to change this state of affairs in a few kitchens.

In recent times, the beanfield has also become emblematic not of ancient civilisations, but of modern civilisation's thin facade of liberty.

On Saturday June 1, 1985, a "peace convoy" of 80–120 vehicles carrying "New Age" travellers, was prevented from getting to Stonehenge to prepare summer solstice celebrations by a police blockade. Wiltshire police went down the line of vehicles systematically smashing windows, dragging out inhabitants and battering them with truncheons. Many of the convoy attempted to escape, within and without their vans, via the adjacent field of ripening fava beans. Police were quick to respond, and travellers' blood fertilised the Salisbury Plain soil in an unprovoked carnage that became known as "The Battle of The Beanfield".

The miners' strike had just ended – a dispute in which the government granted the police new powers and carte blanche to use any repressive means at their disposal in the war against what Thatcher termed "the enemy within". First the trade unionists, then the travellers. Both movements may indeed have been enemies of the Thatcher project; both, in different ways, proffered a practical vision of an alternative, fairer society; neither have fully recovered from the intense campaign against them in the 1980s.

The Battle of the Beanfield, like the Battle of Orgreave[38], was a sad day for human beans, and the utopian whiff of broad beans is there to remind us of it.

Carrot Gold

June 30, 2011

"If you assume there's no hope, you guarantee that there will be no hope. If you assume that there is an instinct for freedom, there are opportunities to change things, there's a chance you may contribute to making a better world. That's your choice."- Noam Chomsky

The realm of possibilities is a shrinking territory unless you periodically push back the boundaries by doing what you suspect you can't do. Ten years ago, OrganicLea was shakily founded on the basis of some half-baked idea of nurturing a local food economy in north-east London. Now the dream has been called into being: only through reflecting on such transformations from fiction to fact can we find it in ourselves to dream new, equally wet-behind-the-ears, dreams.

On a different – literally fundamental – scale, this year we've grown carrots. The carrot family are the awkward squad of the veg pack. Some people claim they can't grow parsnips. In lore, only witches can grow parsley, and during the witch-hunts – to do so brought charges of witchcraft.

As for me, for some time I've maintained that carrots are my bogey crop. My first few enthusiastic attempts failed due to the poor and slow germination characteristic of them and their aforementioned cousins. And, whether in Yorkshire or London, I've always gardened on heavy clay, which for root crops must feel something like wading through treacle, with consequently stunted results. There's a reason most commercial carrots are raised in sandy areas.

But one interesting outcome of crop rotations is that every year you end up growing things that wouldn't be your first choice, because you have to somehow fill that allocated space in the planting plan. Like painting with a limited palette, this apparent restriction can in fact open doors we would otherwise keep shut: for example, some of our weirdest salad leaf discoveries have arisen from the constant quest to find leaves to grow that are not in the three key salad families.

I find it a peculiar fact, but a fact it is, that the good folk of Waltham Forest will only eat so much celery. So this year, with trepidation, we sowed our first roots – carrots – into the second *Apiaceae* bed in the Entrance Field. In mitigation, we went for "Chantenay Red Cored", a thick, short-rooted cultivar.

It's not been a great year for the orange pointy things: the drought of April/May has wrecked a whole generation's germination in their East Anglian heartland. Our sowings have had a battle too, but last week, when we pulled for them, they rose up: chunky, glowing, earthy and bunchworthy; a triumph of hope.

Relaying the News and the Olds

June 11, 2012

It's taken a little time, but we're now closing in on the dream where the harvesting schedule is an endless, effortless relay, one seasonal delight pouring forth just as one fades away. This year the rhubarb has run over to spring garlic; up sprung the asparagus, and as their shoots leave, in stream the strawberries. In the near distance be the broad beans; on the summer solstice horizon, Bull's Blood beetroot. Then we're into the glowing days of abundance, then the autumn harvest festival, then the winter brassicas: all underpinned by year-round salad leaves.

It is the first year of cropping asparagus, but the strawberry fruit are on their way to becoming a familiar feature. On Friday, on cue – two weeks after laying the mulch and one week after netting, almost as if we'd planned it – the first ripe pick. Forty-mph winds lashed the rain against us, a far cry from the good-day sunshines of fruit-picking memory. A third of the crop had to be chucked or consumed at point of pick: slugs and botrytis all too active in this weather, which has also watered down the flavour somewhat. Still, after the storm, what a gift: crates of bright red summer stacked in the warehouse, reeking of goodly sweetness. I was found with my head over the punnets, snorting them: Stefan suggested charging ten pence a sniff. They're probably worth more.

The perennials and glasshouse crops are growing apace, but these long cooling off periods are stalling the outdoor delights. Field cultivations continue to be aborted as heavy rain makes the soil unworkable. The Entrance Field has been a meadow or pasture for at least two and a half centuries, probably more: it is likely part of the medieval *halke* – nook or enclosure – in the *wood*, that gave Hawkwood its name. The Field and its company of grasses are old, old friends, and it will take us many carrots and sticks to persuade it that flowering plants are generally preferable. Weeding the grass out of the Field is, at the best of times, the horticultural equivalent of painting the Forth Bridge. Right now from our place of resignation, it's more like the Bridge of Sighs.

That's the thing about old relationships: they take a long time to make, and a longer time to break. The strawberries are nippers to the grass, but they are already beginning to belong here. The fan-trained peaches and gages are starting to fit, and tomatoes and beans form the default summer skyline. The community market garden is coming home.

Games Without Frontiers

June 21, 2012

Out there, the big summer of sport is just hotting up, but at Hawkwood our sports season is at its climax. In the Race to the Sky, Jo and Jairo's climbing bean selections are ahead neck and neck, or rather, apical shoot and apical shoot. It will literally go to the wire: that is, the top wire of the glasshouse apex. Following their progress day by day has been pretty exciting.

Then on Wednesday, the third annual Horticultural Games took place. There were some outstanding performances, with Nicole shredding the women's world record for Salad Tossing, and John coming from nowhere to win the Potato & Knife (a plant-based alternative to Egg & Spoon). In the overall team competition, the Vines lifted the flower pot trophy, despite stiff competition from the Fruit, the Vegetables, and the Salad Team, who held on to their Tug of Peace title with nonviolent determination. At the end of the day, as they say, it was the Big Team of OrganicLea that won: coop members, volunteer workers and course participants, coming together to celebrate midsummer – one of the two most important days in the Gardening Calendar.

Next to this very particular playfulness, professional sport seems seriously abstracted. Yet most games began this way: as seasonal, local recreation that often demonstrated and developed skills and strengths that were useful to society. Athletics is based on Greek military training; early bike racers came from the massed ranks of cycle porters and couriers; and village football was a veiled rehearsal for rioting.

A while ago that beautiful magazine *The Land* envisaged a future where the Olympics had mutated into the "Global Village Games", with international scything and squash growing contests replacing the current "pointless acts of physical prowess". Soon, the Lea Valley will be polarised: on the lower banks, a unique territory of natural regeneration and surviving manufacturing industry has been flattened into a placeless setting for two weeks of corporate-dominated athletic spectacle. It will be busy and vibrant. The security forces will see it is safe, whatever the cost.

Upstream, you might still find that sense of gentle liberty – of stewarded wildness and ad hoc leisure pursuits that characterise England's waterways and commons. Chuck a right and you might find a glasshouse where everyone's beans touch the stars, and cyclists load their trailers with landrace tomatoes[39].

If you ask me there's no contest.

Anyone for Squash?

June 11, 2013

It doesn't seem to take all that much in the end. After all the dreaming and scheming – all the sweat and worry and tears – just a bit of love and care and then, when finally Warmth and Light arrive, muttering their apologies and looking slightly shifty, everything else just falls into place: *plants grow by themselves.*

It was a rollover year for the great Hawkwood Bean Sweepstake, as last year everyone's Big French Ones stopped short of the two-metre high top wire. This year, it was over in a flash: well, a fortnight. A young "Neckargold" stalk, backed by an only-slightly-older-but-much-smaller Ronan, aged six months, shot to success, bagging Ronan the £17 jackpot. Summer's youth: a long takes a little time.

Still far to go though. A full four weeks after planting, the squashes in the Entrance Field are only starting to suggest an interest in "getting away", much to my relief, as we did the BIG planting of squash, across the whole of the Old Kitchen Garden, on that cool damp Wednesday last week.

One way or another, this year will be a squashy one. As well as its moment in the "all or nothing" Kitchen Garden rotation, there are four beds in the Entrance Field, plus we're trailing some, Tuscan-style, through the vineyard.

As is *The Rule* here, we've gone largely for tried and tested cultivars: the rich orange "Uchiki Kuri"; the dense, chestnutty "Buttercup"; "Sweet Dumpling", our lovable tagine grenade; and "Blue Ballet", which is as weirdly gracious as it sounds. New entries for this year are the ornate eye-candy of "Turks Turban"; the naked seeded "Retzer Gold"; the heritage wild card and Billy Bragg favourite "New England Sugar Pie"; the elf-sized "Jack Be Little". And of course there's "Hawkwood Hybrid", the first step on our journey to breeding a wonderful Waltham Forest winter squash.

There's more to this breeding lark than meets the eye. During high-level roast vegetable meetings Sean and I decided that, while the butternut persists in being the nation's favourite squash, it is inferior in flavour, keeping quality and comical wartiness, to something like a "Green Hokkaido". The simple act of marrying Hokkaido and Butternut, then, would, if not change the world, look forward to a New England. As Thomas Jefferson said, "the greatest service which can be rendered any country is to add a useful plant to its culture".

The useful plant we've added at this point is not a better-flavoured butternut, but a bastard that looks and tastes nothing like either parent, and is twice their size. We've created a monster, albeit a tasty one. With scary inevitability, scientific progress presses on this season, as I attempt to inbreed two Hawkwood Hybrids in the confinement of the East Wing of the glasshouse. We have a long way to go before we can release a stable, open-pollinated OrganicLea variety on a world that didn't ask for it in the first place. But somehow what started as a sideline summer shenanigan may be becoming a life's work.

I suppose that feeling – that despite a project being neither wanted, needed or requested by anyone, there is somehow no turning back — is something that the biotech people can relate to, but that's where the similarities end. The new EU "Plant Reproductive Material Law" is the latest naked, vindictive attack on home gardeners and small growers by the biotech corporations pursuing a stranglehold on the very stuff of life. Quite where it leaves us, with the Hawkwood Hybrid and our living library of heritage beans and tomatoes, I've still yet to fathom, though it's likely to be, if not on, then close to, a sticky wicket, much like the rest of the planet.

Squashes remain a beacon of hope amidst such corporate control freakery. They are the very picture of promiscuous, rampant diversity. The vision of our stalls and stores cascading in nine contrasting shapes, shades and sizes at the end of summer is as liberating as it is seductive. It's now approaching midsummer though, and all we have to show for this vision, all our work so far, is a few pale green leaves on the ground. Now back to nature.

Strawberries are Here: It's Love All

June 24, 2013

I don't follow the Chinese calendar – I can barely keep up with my personal diary – but if I had to guess, I'd suppose that this is the Year of the Tortoise. Still to pick up any apparent momentum after an excruciatingly slow start, somehow it *is getting there*. People are moaning about the "lack of summer" (as if we ever, or would ever, not moan if we had three months of unbridled heatwave). But summer IS HERE, only it's shuffled in so cautiously most of us haven't noticed yet.

People who work outdoors tend to notice these things quicker, which is surely only a fair trade-off for having to spend so much time appreciating, first freezing hand, how bloody cold winter actually is. Mind, there are more bright heavenly days in winter, Horatio, than are dreamt of in warmed offices.

John, Paul and I couldn't fail to notice it on Friday: we were on the first strawberry pick. A full month later than 2011's, but the commencing of the trawling of British Summer's flagship berry on the very day of the summer solstice seemed spot on. What's more, once again, our strawbs are ripe in time for Wimbledon. In an age when virtually all of the UK's commercial strawberry production has been pulled indoors – and worse, clear of the soil – it makes me proud, very proud, to be raising sweet red joy from our cold hard clay, in the western winds, in time for the opening day of the summer fruits and sports season.

Regular spectators will know that the highlight of the summer sports season here at Hawkwood are the midsummer Horticultural Games. This year, the day was glorious in every way. With over 70 in attendance, Adam, freshly returned from representing the newly-formed UK Landworkers' Alliance at the quadrennial Via Campesina Conference in Jakarta, hurled his way into history with a win in the Men's Salad Tossing. Jo avoided the spectacular pile-up at the finish of the Sack Race to grab a plant pot trophy for the otherwise underachieving Fruit Team. The big upset was that the Weight Lifting – a discipline of strength and skill, where contestants, having lifted the garlic dumbbell must go on to guess its weight – was won not by any of the stall workers, box scheme packers or harvest hands, but Brian, our mere Funding & Council Liaison Officer.

For once, the Potato & Knife Race was not marred by revelations or accusations of "thumbing" by leading athletes, and Ippy (Team Salad) was a worthy winner in the Women's event. The Tug of Peace was high drama indeed: the passion and grit with which participants in the Final heaved for Vines and Vegetables was moving. In the end, the Vines Team, as Marlene said, pipped it, and in doing so prised the overall Team Trophy. Fitting, in a year when the first grape harvest is due to enter a newly fitted cooperative Winery.

The Hawkwood Games, then, and its lesser relation the Wimbledon Lawn Tennis Championship, are trumpeted as heralding the red-letter start of the summer fruit season. What's less considered is that every start starts with an end, or is it every end ends with a start? I always get muddled. Anyway, the point being that in the endless breath-taking rally between seasonal superfoods, strawberries bounce up exactly where rhubarb and asparagus leave off.

So on Tuesday, there was a subtle poignancy with which Vi hung the asparagus knife back up for the good; and when Gary weighed out the last bundle of crimson sticks, I was half expecting the credits to start rolling. Sad, but right: the early excitement of each delicacy has worn off: no rhubarb whatsoever sold on our stalls last week. And the crop is equally tired of being picked. It's their time to grow unchecked. So on we go…

Starts and ends, leaving things behind and taking things forward, was the theme beautifully addressed by our Outreach Worker Liz, in the solstice ritual she devised for the post-Games after-party for coop members and trainees. The plant world, and so our lives, turn on subtle, tortoise-like shifts, punctuated by the occasional Big Leap. This time is closer to the latter.

It's by no means perfect, but this is our summer. So go forth and taste good, local, organic, love-grown strawberries, wherever they may be.

Across the Gulf
of Strawberries

June 8, 2014

One of the key principles of ecology, and thus ecological food growing, is that of relationships. It's not just what's there, it's how what's there interacts with what's around it and its habitat, that creates an ecosystem. Unfortunately, relationships are harder than things to "show and tell" on site tours: the intricate web of microbial life in the soil, and the web of connections between the people and land that produce the food, and those that eat it, can only be gesticulated at in a dramatic but slightly vague manner.

This is one reason why reductive science – science that looks at stuff, but not how stuff connects with other stuff – has held so much sway in agriculture and other areas. The times are a-changing, though it's not clear what into: even the Big Boys like Tesco and McDonalds are starting to respond to customers' need to feel a sense of connection with the source of their food, and now assault us with phoney "meet our farm" images on their billboards and juggernauts.

Real relationships are not only often invisible, they're also complex, volatile, take time and are held in trust: all things that don't show up too well on the balance sheet and are, it has to be said, a pretty inconvenient way of running things, though it's hard to work out who to file that particular complaint with. In our work with London restaurants we try to build up a partnership deeper than a mere buyer/ seller encounter, through means such as weekly conversations, reciprocal visits and direct delivery or "short supply chains".

What we find is that our relationship "with a restaurant" can often be very personal, and rest on a relationship with a key chef. The "Camden bicycle run", which spearheaded our external distribution strategy when we started out, has gone the way of lemonade, Coca-Cola and Newcastle Brown Ale: despite the name, it now has no Camden whatsoever left in it. Our cooks have slung their hooks and recipe books to other nooks and pantries, and our trade with their old kitchen hasn't stayed. The bicycle delivery route, now performed by our friends Bike Box with our Christiania trailers, goes on strong, but King's Cross, Euston and Islington Run doesn't sound half as cool.

On the ground, one of the team formations we use for managing the vegetable beds is the "pincer movement" or "working towards each other". It's an especially useful manoeuvre when it comes to light weeding or ripe-pick harvesting. Strawberry season is now upon us. It always appears that way, ambushing from above. Summer still surprises. Nicely: strawberries have always never looked, smelt, tasted, so fresh.

Anyway, as a tactic the pincer is simple and elegant. The beds in the Entrance Field are mostly sixty metres, those in the Old Kitchen Garden thirty-four, subdivided by the Middle Way path that runs either up it or down it, depending on whether you take the side of the hawthorn or the lime tree. One pair starts either side of the far end of the bed, the other from the near end. Working towards each other. When we meet, the bed is complete, prompting a greeting, sometimes a hand shake, a hugless embrace. What I call a "Channel Tunnel Moment".

Those of my generation may remember the scene. French workers drilled a hole from Calais, British ones from the white cliffs, all the way deep under twenty-one miles of Big Blue. By some improbable feat the drillings met up, in good time, somewhere round the middle, and TV footage showed the miners shaking hands though the little joining. It was a unifying image: while the primary motivation for the building of the Chunnel was business, there could be no denying the haunting hope for humanity in this interracial meeting and greeting. It showed that people were capable of tearing down obstacles between them, like the Berlin Wall, and also of building – bridges and tunnels – across divides, physical and cultural.

Last week, UKIP's xenophobic message of despair polled well in the European elections[40], and the spirit of that Channel Tunnel Moment may seem more distant. But pitching despair against despair will yield one certain result. Better still, in all we do, to keep working towards each other. Making the most of the strawberries along the way.

Paul Robeson Sings

June 25, 2014

"Life is what happens to you when you're busy making other plans", quoth John Lennon. Summer is life, a high note singing on a breeze; the Longest Day happens quickly.

This year, we marked this midsummer moment with a Permaculture Introduction course and gathering at Dial House[41], an autonomous space that reappears on numerous branches of OrganicLea's extended family tree; and the traditional solstice celebration and horticultural games. In the latter, the Fruit Team's triumph was long awaited and fitting, for nothing says summer like ripe soft fruits.

Queen Crimson of the fruits is the strawberry, the picking of which has been as frenzied as ever over the midsummer weeks. This year the run-in to Wimbledon has met a sweet volley of warmth, meaning more time spent plucking into punnets rather than chucking off the rotted and the slugged, an altogether better pursuit. Still, these days the strawberry harvest seems far from a fleeting glory, almost never ending, leading me to ask whether it's sensible to cultivate eight beds of berries: the final answer seems to be yes. People love them; they always go.

Equally loved, picked less frenziedly through a longer, glasshouse window, are the fruits of Lycopersicon esculentum, the tomato. For the first time we have these ripe by the solstice. Just a few, and just one cultivar – "Darby Striped Yellow/ Green" – but that's enough to set the rest of them off, like a pack of howling wolves. This year the howls I'm most looking forward to hearing from are our new varieties, and one in particular, the black tomato "Paul Robeson".

As a human, Paul Robeson, born in 1898, achieved international renown as a singer and actor. His outspoken support for the Republicans in the Spanish Civil War, against racism at home in the States, and his interest in the Soviet Union, led to his blacklisting during the McCarthy era, the revoking of his passport and continued harassment by the FBI. Such persecution by the authorities contributed to the demise of his career and health. He died in Philadelphia in 1976.

Gone but not forgotten. By their fruits shall ye know them[42].

Like so many black tomatoes, "Paul Robeson" hails from the east, bred by Soviet horticulturalists and named in his honour, a tribute to his anti-imperialist stance and his full-bodied baritone. We eat these always in remembrance.[43] His unique relationship with Welsh coal miners, with whom he sang, worked and marched alongside in the 1920s, resurfaced this century in the Manic Street Preachers track "Let Paul Robeson Sing". His signature tune "Ol' Man River" is still known and sung across the world:

"He don' plant tater/ He don' plant cotton/ An' dem dat plants 'em/ Is soon forgotten/ But Ol' Man River/ He jes' keeps rollin' along".

Most importantly, his unfashionable challenging of his home country's apartheid sowed some of the seeds of the civil rights movement, and the rest is history: full political rights, and a level of racial equality and dignity that could only have been dreamt of in Robeson's time.

Some of the seeds sown are producing ripe fruits, but there is still a long way to go. Summer in this green-grey valley, the River Lea rollin' along.

July

Floral Tribute (2012)
Calendula, cornflower, phacelia and mustard brighten up the glasshouse and bring in
the pest predators; young tomato, cucumber and bean plants look on in admiration

On Inspection

July 29, 2010

OrganicLea's Hawkwood Nursery had its first organic inspection a couple of weeks ago. Subject to a little bit of extra paperwork, we are pleased to announce that, as of this time next year, Hawkwood produce will be classed as "in conversion to organic", and the following year can be labelled as organic. Our actual techniques will change very little – as our name suggests, we have always promoted and practised organic gardening. We are Wholesome Food Association affiliated, sell within six miles of our site, and our gates are open for people to come and have a look at how we attempt to produce food by working with nature. So why go to the bother and expense of getting regularly inspected by the Soil Association?

Well, for one thing, organic certification is an independent guarantee to the customer, and as we are beginning to feed people who may not have a long-term relationship with us, for example people who happen to grab a bite at Table 7 restaurant in Chingford, this may be important. Secondly, our partner in East Anglia, Hughes Organics, is certified organic, and it is good for us to be on a "level playing field" with them, and to fully understand the trials and triumphs of having to pass annual inspection and scrutiny.

Third, and relatedly, we become producer members of the Soil Association, who remain an important national voice for sanity in the food system. Important but not imperfect: small growers and community retailers like us, who ultimately are our only hope of really tackling the social-environmental crises facing us, are the pioneers and backbone of the organic movement, but have not always been well served by the leadership in their desire to court big players such as supermarkets and large landowners. OrganicLea is now a fully paid up member of a network of organic producers, on whom any hope for a "future-proof" food system rests heavily. This is what we have to remind ourselves when we next have to send off for permission to use dried seaweed![44]

The previous day, OrganicLea members Clare and Brian took on the role of inspectors – of Mrs. Begum's allotment plot in Leyton. Mrs. B is one of our decentralised *Cropshare* growers who markets her surplus produce through our box scheme and stall, growing in accordance with *Wholesome Food Association* principles.

Then there are the really valuable "inspections" by volunteers and visitors returning after an absence from Hawkwood. Working day by day, you notice the seasons steadily ringing the changes but not the "time lapse" perspective of sporadic encounters. When others are moved to remark how on how good the Entrance Field is looking, or how the cucumbers have grown, it's a Wages Day.

Of course, self-inspection is paramount but easily overlooked in the hustle and bustle of daily industry. I try to walk the site and commune with the flora and fauna once a week. This week I can report that the peppers and celery are well on their way. It feels like we've passed most inspections with the flying colours of high summer.

Short of Water

July 29, 2010

The beetroot, salads, parsley and basil continue to crop apace, as do the outdoor French beans "Borlotto di Fuoco", and the tomatoes, from seed sown in the chilly depths of early March. The cucumbers, after their woodlice-induced false start, have been going to market for the last couple of weeks and are of notably firmer texture and stronger flavour – some might even say more *cucumbery* – than the watery supermarket specimens.

One of the many reasons that small-scale organic produce is often regarded as tasting better is because its flesh is not drowned in water in an attempt to add weight to increase slim profit margins. It's not that irrigation rates are set by organic standards: it's just a spin-off of having in place a grower for whom sustainability, ecology and quality are the raisons d'être. People are often surprised at how little we water at Hawkwood. But, provided the soil is given a thorough soaking once a week (and provided you have a medium to heavy soil with good levels of organic matter) it seems this is usually enough and, as the old adage goes, "enough is as good as a feast". Water too much and you might spoil the plant, or at least the flavour.

That said, ecology is so much fine balances on swings and roundabouts. I am delighted, nay smug, to report the squash and beans swell lusciously despite no watering since they were planted out, bar the measly 95 millimetres the heavens have tossed their way in the last three months. But I must also confess that the unwelcome guest of hot, dry glasshouses, the red spider mite, is starting to make a meal of the tasty cucumbers, and the delicious "Berner Rose" tomatoes are yet to make an appearance at our outlets due to the disfiguring blossom end rot. The latter is an ugly symptom of calcium deficiency, which in turn is a symptom of water shortage, UK soils being virtually never short of calcium.

We control water in the glasshouse, so can begin to remedy these: not so the first early potatoes, left Spartan-like to fend for themselves high and dry at the top of the Entrance Field. The foliage is dying back yet the tubers are stunted by lack of moisture. They'll be fiddly and time-consuming to harvest, likewise to prepare, but I'll bet all the sea round China they're as tasty as any spud on a London plate next week.

The Season So Far

July 20, 2011

Up until now, it's been a fine season. Warm, not too hot; and a decent amount of moisture: after the parched spring, accumulated rainfall has pulled itself back to last year's level. OK, the peppers are asking for more heat, but you can't please all the plants all the time: the temperate field veg is giving good feedback, and the salad leaves are holding up.

Mid to late summer is a difficult patch in the grower-supporter relationship (*supporter* being a preferable term to *customer* when talking about our produce recipients). Just as the lean times give way to abundance, half the people you've grown it for seem to disappear to some far-flung festival or holiday destination.

From the supporters' perspective, the hot months drive a change in palette, in favour of light, cool, "wet" foods: surely, if there was ever a time to relish ultra-fresh local salad leaves, this is it! Yet, this is exactly the moment when I begin issuing dire warnings about the "salad gap" (see August 31, 2010).

This year, thanks to the aforementioned weather conditions, the winter salads should be off to a flyer, while the veterans of spring hold up well. This doesn't mean there won't *be* a salad gap, but with a bit of luck and judgement, it should be narrower and shallower than might be the case.

Meanwhile, our Open Day this month will feature the first of a series of public workshops exploring different ways of preserving "surplus" produce. So perhaps growers and supporters alike will make it through the bumpy patch wasting not and wanting not.

Social Climbers

July 31, 2011

In the Celtic calendar it is Lammas, the festival of the grain harvest and of ripening fruits. This is the time that the garden and glasshouse *should* be at their verdant peak. After a bit of considered gazing around this week, I concluded that, happily, we have risen to that air of abundance.

The tomatoes are coming thick as passata, getting good reviews and flying off whatever stalls we put them on. Now I wish we'd planted more, though if you catch me waxing lyrical about peppers in a month's time, you'll know I've revised this view.

Many gardeners have reported this as a "bad year for beans" (French and runners). The obvious explanation would be that the dry spring left soil moisture levels deficient well into the summer: beans don't ask for much except water. But even our trickle-irrigated glasshouse climbers, and late-planted outdoor dwarves, have been somewhat pest-prone and lacklustre this year. Still, we'll be picking our first French ones this week and I'm expecting a reasonable harvest over the coming month. The "Kew Blue" under glass are finally resplendent, with elegant dark leaves, indigo flowers and deep purple slender pods: even a poor crop would be forgiven in the light of this yield of eye-candy, a trade-off I rarely buy in to.

We'll let them climb, Jack-and-the-Beanstalk-like, above the top wire and through the glass ceiling if they care to. But the tomatoes, cucumbers, melons and gourds are now having their vertical growth terminated at precisely the height at which our six-footers, Ed and Jonny, can reach to pinch. Not long ago I could have lost these plants, like the dream of a community plant nursery, in a gust of ill wind or a tight fist; now they, and the garden they star in, is bigger than me every which way you look at it. Days pass and you find yourself only able to utter the very clichés that elderly relatives annoyed you with as a child: *my, haven't you grown...*

As Good as it Gets

July 5, 2012

At the risk of tempting fate, or any other mysterious force that might catch wind, summer has largely settled here, and the garden grows: grows away from the sorry spring's torrential woes. Almost six months to the day after telling Mary "it doesn't get much worse than this" as we picked chilled salad with frozen hands, I lined up with apprentices Dean and Adam, peered through the riot of companion flowers and onto the verdant greens of youthful glasshouse and field crops, and muttered "this is as good as it gets."

Both statements are a shadow of the truth. Winter has its share of comforts and joys, of course; all seasons, all days, have their moments of paradise, their hours of grind. Yet, all things being equal, the garden in early summer is at its most alive: lush spring leaf overlaps with fresh summer flowers and exuberant ripe fruits: no other time can hold these three crucial ingredients in such measure.

Our early fruits are strawberries and broad beans (the latter are, after all, fruiting vegetables). And this week's harvest will be as bumper as any other this year: the autumn beans have been caught by the spring sown stock; the maincrop strawberries reached the red of the earlies: all round, a time of crescendo. We are very grateful to Inspiral and Growing Communities for giving us an outlet for the abundance, and saving us from the unthinkable: crops rotting "on the vine".

Both are time-consuming to pick, something I perhaps should have considered when I plumped for filling the Old Kitchen Garden with broad beans when plotting the planting plan in the depths of December, but hey. To be up early doors on a fine summer's morn, or even a damp one, as the birds begin to find their voice; a flask of coffee, some friends, and more beans than I've ever eaten. Moments like this.

From Weather Systems to Food Systems

July 16, 2012

Within the last week, two of the farmers I have the most time for – Gerald Miles in Wales and Iain Tolhurst in Berkshire – have cited this as the worst growing season in living memory. These are long (thirty to forty years apiece) and detailed memories. Mine is shorter and almost as cloudy as our spring/ summer: the sun has rarely fully shone, the rain never convincingly abated. Hopefully 02012[45] will go down as a terrible year rather than the start of a terrible trend, though Tolhurst observes that "extreme weather events" have been occurring at closer intervals over the last decade. August or September may bring a reprieve; who knows? Certainly not the meteorologists and weather pundits, who seem to have found the whole thing as unfathomable as the rest of us.

Given all this, we feel doubly blessed with what we have achieved so far at Hawkwood. Despite the inevitable slow growth, and the equally inevitable boom in slugs and rots, the land has poured forth a steady stream of salad, some fine asparagus, and just recently nigh on a tonne of saleable broad beans and strawberries: enough to kill you if they landed on your head in an extreme weather event of biblical proportions. This in a year when the asparagus festival was cancelled, industrial UK strawberry production plummeted, and in some areas of the Old Kitchen Garden 90 per cent of the crop had to be abandoned for slugs to finish what they started.

Not a great time to be doing local food, you might say. On the other hand, in tough times like these, time and again the small-scale and diverse systems have been shown to have many advantages over operations that are machine-dependent and/ or monocultures. The dull, wet conditions have not benefitted our tomatoes, but they've kept the salad leaves unseasonably green and fresh; London gardeners can at least get onto their slug-ridden allotments, while commercial growers who use tractors for every cultivation can only fidget indoors until the soil dries.

Last weekend 140 people came to Hawkwood to explore possibilities for building a food sovereignty movement in the UK. Food sovereignty as a concept developed from attempts in the global south to voice a positive alternative to food security, encapsulating "the right of peoples to healthy and culturally-appropriate food produced through ecologically sound and sustainable methods, and their right to define their own food and agricultural systems" (Declaration of Nyeleni 2007).

In many ways this is the realisation of an elusive dream for OrganicLea – community gardeners, global justice campaigners, producers and food activists coming together to form a tangible alliance for "Transforming Our Food System". A small step on a world-changing journey, but by Tuesday something had already changed. Picking through slug-damaged beans, on your knees, in the rain, is the kind of work that could make you question what on earth you're doing with your life. In the wake of the gathering, though, it felt like vital work: part of a movement, a wider struggle.

If, as appears to be the case, we can't gain democratic control of the weather, democratic control of food production and distribution has to be the next best thing.

Tomatoes, and the Triumph of Hope

July 24, 2012

I've made mention here before of how, in the garden calendar, every week witnesses an annual event, a holy day, so that the garden seems to become the venue for a series of small festivals. Last week saw the Last Week of the Strawberries, but before the glittering red decorations were down, the garlic was brought in, decking the glasshouse with its muddy white ribbons.

Even in this gloomy growing season, the regular harvest festivals serve to lift the spirits and bring reasons to be cheerful: the possibilities of redemption whatever the weather. In this gloomy growing season, the more reason for smiles and small celebrations as we greet the slow, but blessedly sure, fruition of beetroot, cucumber, French beans, tomatoes. And the greatest of these is tomatoes.

What is it with the British and their tomatoes? For a Central American plant long regarded as a poisonous (due to its membership of the nightshade family) ornamental, and only admitted into full culinary citizenship during the second world war, it is surprisingly central to our food and gardening culture. When it comes to flying off the shelves – or rather, sliding off the grocers' grass – of our market stalls, they beat all comers, even strawbs. The same is true for our plant sales: in London it seems every gardener of every culture is somehow compelled to raise a few toms. And also non-gardeners: in so many urban yards and balconies, the "love apple", or "wolf peach", as it has been variously known, is the only cultivated plant on show, in grow bags, pots, or rare squares of ground.

In a bad year – of which 2012 is an outstanding example – the plants might give few ripe fruit even, and green tomato chutney will be the only order of the day. For this reason I, perhaps dogmatically, regard them as an "indoor crop". Conversely, perhaps, this riskiness gives an extra frisson that makes planting some "Gardeners Delight" even more irresistible. Perhaps, after all, we all *live* in hope.

There is *nothing* remotely frisson about Blight appearing on our Black Russians in early July, though I suppose the premature presence of this awful disease will result in greater rejoicing for every week of surviving tomato fruitfulness hence. Amongst our other heritage cultivars this year are local heroes "Kondine Red" (see March 6, 2010) and "Essex Wonder" (see March 2, 2011); "Garden Peach"; "Tiger Tom"; and "Carter's Golden Sunrise".

"Tiger Tom" is an early, good cropper with attractive stripes, which wins many of our taste tests, striking a near-perfect balance between acidity and sweetness. "Carter's Golden Sunrise", a bright yellow orb, tastes like tomatoes used to. It was raised by Carter's of Raynes Park, London, in the 1890s, when the ubiquitous popularity of this odd, blight-prone, cold-intolerant plant can barely have been

123

imagined possible. But other worlds *are* possible, beyond this climate chaos and other symptoms of our social and environmental malaise: there truly is hope in the nightshade.

The Whole Harvest

July 5, 2013

"Some busy 'gin to team the loaded corn / Which night throng'd round the barns becrouded door / Such plentious scenes the farmers yards adorn / Such busy bustling toils now mark the harvest morn." - John Clare, The Harvest Morning

How to finish? Sometimes I feel like my life is but a series of short stories all with mildly disappointing conclusions, whether the backdrop is a bicycle race, a political campaign, or a gardening workshop. The art of finishing is one I can only hope to become proficient in before I go.

At least I'm not alone: none of us are born finishers, and few get to finishing school. Perhaps this is why harvesting – the grower's finale – isn't given half the head space or page inches of other gardening techniques, such as the ever ongoing struggles of weed, pest and disease management. When I offer to show someone how we harvest chard, it's not uncommon to be looked upon with an expression of amusement and pity. Because, *you just pick it, right?* What's to talk about?

In fact, amongst leaf growers, there is considerable debate as to the true, righteous way to pick chard, and the jury is out as to whether we've found it at Hawkwood. There is, though, broad consensus as to the range of considerations to be taken into account. These include: maintaining turgor; losing field heat; entry points for disease; contamination with soil; quality control; size of leaf; patterns of movement across the bed; rogueing out; inclusion or exclusion of other maintenance operations; proportion of chard to other leaves if picking for the salad mix; policy on bolting plants; handling minimisation; tool selection; fiddliness thresholds; and choice of cycling methods for grade outs.

Needless to say, even just touching on this smorgasbord of issues makes for a bewildering induction, bordering on an alarming one, if you just happen to have volunteered yourself to pick chard as it was a job that needed doing and sounded pretty straightforward, and in any case you don't care too much for chard anyway.

This is where Tuesday's Harvest Hands come in. It's a crack squad of skilled pickers, consisting, this Harvest Moon, of (clockwise, from far left): Adam; the Trainee Trio of Aimée, Kristen and Paul; Apprentice Gary; Jonny the Rt. Hon. Secretary for Salad; Kate; Naeema; Frank; and Paul Senior. I think that's me behind Adam, looking quizzically at a chard leaf. The work is hard, and also a celebration. In the ever ongoing struggle of growing, this is *what it means to win*: a full trough of salad and crates of strawberries stacked up in the packing bay. All the sweat and toil, all the brain and muscle energy, find a culmination here. On Harvest Tuesdays, a bowl of decorated salad is laid on the altar of the lunch table to honour this. Not in the text books, but in the songs and festivals of the land, the harvest is central.

So we are in festival season: strawberries and salad are literally growing faster than we can pick them, the beans are ripening on the vine, and the fat beets will kick into their sweet song next week. Routine maintenance never ceases, but there is an active shift from nurturing to gathering. The Spring Lean eats our dust.

Another kind of harvest was celebrated at our Open Day last Sunday. "I found the poems in the fields / And only wrote them down"[46], quoth John Clare (1793–1864), a ploughboy who harvested his poems from the nature around his village of Helpston, Northamptonshire, and for a few years of his life, in the very Epping Forest that embraces Hawkwood.

His words chronicle the richness of the rural land and life, and the process of its impoverishment by The Enclosures, or what we might now call land grabs. His labours were not entirely in vain: his was not a final defeat. The poems provide information and inspiration for the work of reconnecting people and land today.

So, to mark Clare's birthday, the day closed with readings, and the unveiling of a John Clare memorial, beautifully etched by Ian, at the pinnacle of a brimming Entrance Field, under the shade of the old oak, a spot dubbed Poets' Corner after its contemplative aspect. A good place to finish.

Common Scents

July 23, 2013

So much to write about, so little time. The last three weeks have been hotter than a Bradford curry and as dry as Yorkshire wit, bringing everything on in lamb leaps and shire-horse bounds. The strawberries ripened too rapidly, shortening the season and causing many to be left fermenting on the plant. Only too late did I recall the virtues of shade cloth for slowing down growth: it seems like a lifetime since we last had need to call on it.

Its dense green weave now drapes over most of the salad plants on the West Bank Terrace, as we try to brake lettuces' urge to flower and reproduce once it gets into the 30s. Indoors, we work with Leaves Who Love The Sun: the tropical basils, amaranths, Malabar spinach, purslane, ice lettuce. Their exotic, soft, sweet flavour and textures have changed the vibe of the salad bags irrevocably.

The Hungry Gap has exploded, and this week salad, strawbs, basil, beetroot, broad beans, French beans, new potatoes, blackcurrants, cut flowers, celery, cucumbers, courgettes and tomatoes are all there for the taking. The growing pains and worries are a memory: our concerns now surround channelling the water flow to where it's most urgently needed; casting shade; keeping ourselves cool, protected and hydrated; finding happy homes for the harvest; and conjuring up time to pick it all. There's much to shout about.

So many strawberries, so short a season: yet the fallen fruits are not wholly wasted. Their sweet super-ripe fragrance follows you around the Entrance Field like, well, a bad smell. All over London, wherever flowering plants are tolerated or encouraged, similar heady oils are driving back the stench of the City: honeysuckle consuming garden fences; meadowsweet wafting across the "wastes" of Walthamstow Marshes; Victoria Park's perfumery of petunias. The world is inverted, nature rising to the top again.

"Smell and memory are both processed in the same ancient area of our brain", observes Richard Mabey in The Perfumier and the Stinkhorn. This must be why summer resonances swim so certainly on the garden's tugging currents of vegetable smells at this time. The umami tang of pinched tomato stems; the crisp suggestion of a suddenly sliced cucumber; basil's holy tones: all these now sizzle and echo through the glasshouse and pack house, excavating old recollections, and laying down new ones. So much to smile about, all the time.

Tamed

July 9, 2014

The spasm that is our strawberry season is over, four weeks and two hundred and eighty kilos later, leaving me feeling much like I felt after England's World Cup exit: anguished and relieved. There is a transcending vibe of relief coupled with joy, though, in all we do at the minute. Every year, as the growing season enters my peripheral senses, I worry that climate change will have hit the point of no return: that we'll be dealt mild damp summers followed by mile damp winters, ad nauseam, and that The Seasons, that elemental pattern that brings the organic grower such happiness and possibilities, will be consumed forever in the oil of greed. This year, not for the first or last time, nature has given us another chance, and with such grace.

The Entrance Field isn't as complete as I'd like by high summer, and sadly we can't blame the weather or the businessmen for this, just self-induced hiccups in planning and propagation. On the other hand, this has given us, and our bee brethren, the unplanned wonder of the wave of azure flowers of the bolted Treviso chicory. The salads are strong and untired, the "tropical salads" in the glasshouse looking especially at home in what for us mortal humans is wilting heat. Growth in this area has been impressive across the board: the annual Bean Sweepstake ended in a dead heat, all our climbing Borlottis crossing the two metre high-wire finish line on the same weekend. Photo finish technology was not something we imagined necessary to install, though I am pondering whether to erect cricket nets to prevent these intrepid clamberers breaking through the glass ceiling.

The cucumbers also started pouring over the top this week, and Aimée, Hannah and I started trying to coax them down again on our weekly tomato and cucumber training rounds. The former are throwing out side shoots less vigorously now: they've taken shape and the fruits are changing traffic lights where we've pruned back the lower branches. So we are approaching that point at which, in our East Anglian partner Grahame Hughes' words, "the tomatoes are tamed".

The Taming of the Tomatoes is a memorable concept, but one I've struggled with over the years. While on the one hand it sums up what a gardener does to plants quite niftily, on the other, like many I see problems caused by the extent to which the wild and free have been forced to the far periphery of the modern world, and regard organic farms and gardens as wildlife corridors back into our homes and hearts.

A reading from *The Little Prince* at Annie and Ben's wedding last weekend finally saw me at ease, possibly helped by the Prosecco:

"I cannot play with you", the fox said, "I am not tamed".

[Little Prince:] "What does that mean — tame?"

"It is an act too often neglected", said the fox. "It means to establish ties. If you tame me, then we shall need each other. To me, you will be unique in all the world. To you, I shall be unique in all the world..."

"I am beginning to understand", said the Little Prince. "There is a flower...I think she has tamed me..."

Our heritage tomatoes, saved from seed year on year, sown from seed in freezing February, potted on, fed on Hawkwood compost and London clay, pinched and supported to dizzy heights and lights, are unique in all the world.

Fine summer days; tomatoes: these things have a way of reworking the ties, bringing us back. Taming us.

Sunshine and Pain

July 27, 2014

I entered into food politics when I began to get an inkling of the crashing waves of hurt involved in feeding people. Now, as a food producer, I believe more than ever that there can be no justification for the suffering inherent in factory farming. I also accept that, for farmer and farmed, there has to be some pain in this game, even in the most compassionate of growing systems.

The worcesterberry thicket fruited well this year, and for those of us sent from the scorching fields to scrape our arms along the thorns for the small claret-blooded berries, the scratches have only just mellowed into the sunburn. In fairness, we were warned: every Rosaceae has its thorn. To look at, you wouldn't imagine that cucumbers were an equally uncomfortable plant to work with. Yet they are, and work with them we must: so much pruning and training do the crawling gourds require. The bristly leaves and stems are a real irritant, especially in the already prickly heat of the close glasshouse. The cool, soothing fruit are the antidote and the reward of course, but I wonder, if I was working full-time in the cucumber houses of the Lea Valley rather than cultivating a couple of beds here, whether I might look on them more like how Benjamin the donkey regards his tail in *Animal Farm*: "he would say that God had given him a tail to keep the flies off, but that he would sooner have had no tail and no flies".

The gargantuan garlic haul happened gloriously last week. It's our key crop this year – having its time in the limelight of the Old Kitchen Garden rotation. Eight thousand pale bulbs now repose, curing, in the glasshouse, exhaling potently. Like all the grand harvests – olives, apples, corn – the "bringing in" of the Kitchen Garden's bulk crop is a beautiful, communal event, culminating in a splendid harvest display. But it doesn't happen at the click of a mouse: many hands laboured to prise the withering stems out from the tangle of undersown clover and trefoil, poised amongst which were the sharp traps of young nettle seedlings. Those who work the land well know the blood, sweat and tears that translate into its pleasing produce; and the joy, laughter, conversation and dreams.

I've noticed that the more sensible people wear sleeves, gloves and hats against nature's more abrasive side. I generally don't. I have a wasteful habit of sleepwalking through the day, and prickles serve to wake me up, remind me of the thrills and shrills of living. Further up the path, the lingering worcesterberry piercings and stinging nettle tattoos keep alive the pick of the week. The senses sometimes need a hand to match the intensity of activity. The plants we've coddled and cuddled and planted carefully in puddles are all grown up now, and in control: they give out leaf, stem and fruit as they see fit. We follow behind: picking, pruning, feigning to keep up. Every season is awe and fascination but in the temperate world, summer, I think of you as my mountaintop. The peak of the growing season, so much crescends on this. We are of mountains once again.

Sure as night follows day, at this moment of unbridled solar power we set to sowing and planting of the winter salads, and summer joy casts its own shadows of sadness. Jo, Clare and Sarah fought hard in defence of one of our volunteers, a refugee, who has been moved out to distant Devon: partial victory, a partial defeat. We should be glad that, alongside the work of growing people and plants, there are those amongst us willing and able to take on such battles beyond. Each little bit adds up, to the taking away of a world of pain.

August

That Glut Feeling

August 17, 2010

It's the days of gluts. On allotments up and down the country, courgettes and bolting lettuces are being chucked onto compost heaps, or desperately thrust at relatives and into jam jars.

It might be argued that a skilled grower should be able to plan their planting and cropping schedules so as to avoid that heart-sinking feeling of nurturing plants to their prime only to realise that no one is expecting them. But it seems that the most experienced, acclaimed organic growers are every bit as gluttonous as the rest of us. One thing we all learn is that, what with all the weather and pestilence out there, it really makes sense to sow much more than you plan to reap. Bad things sometimes happen. The good news is, they often don't.

Our main glut right now is basil. It needed some persuading to get growing in the glasshouse ground in early May, but it's now a sight and smell to behold. With its brilliant green, glossy, convex leaves, the stand of bushes has a discernible aura; and when it's picked for the stall on Friday, the crushing of stems release its incense throughout the building: close your eyes and you could imagine yourself in a kind of food-worshippers' temple. Open them again.

However, the basil is looking so great partly because we're not pruning it back as hard as we need to, to prolong the leafy stage of its life. Fortunately, there is the "Ethical Eats" network of food businesses, brought together by Sustain, the alliance for better food and farming[47]. A call out to them yielded a healthy response rate. As a result, for the first time Hawkwood produce is being traded outside of Waltham Forest and the Lea Valley bioregion – to Hackney's Happy Kitchen, Islington's The Alma, and Camden's Manna restaurant. Not only has this ensured that one of the finest "Sweet Genovese" beds in London does not go to waste (though at least recycling nutrients via the compost heap means it's never a *total* waste), it has also provided an opportunity to meet three more independent caterers who share our passion for *good* food, in its widest sense, and who we may develop a longer-term, mutually beneficial relationship with.

So, for all the worry, gluts have this social function too: for us, as for all the allotmenteers, they're an opportunity to branch out, share, make friends – to forge community.

Mind the Gap

August 31, 2010

People accustomed to eating seasonally are at least familiar with the term "Hungry Gap" – that period in early summer where last year's stores run bare before the new season crops are ready to bring in. The term refers to the "staples": potatoes, carrots, onions, apples; but the vast majority of our fruit and veg has its season, and, conversely, its own "gap".

Small-scale growers like us have begun to master the art of all-year-round salad leaves, as the public begins to welcome this fresh handout of winter vitamins. This is done by gradually replacing ageing lettuce, mibuna, etc, throughout the spring and summer, thus ensuring a steady supply of an ever-evolving mix. This is fairly straightforward, or rather would be if I was more organised, but the winter salads are a bit trickier.

You see, in the UK there is a *growing season*, and therefore a growing *gap*. Put simply and starkly, nothing bothers to grow much for a good five months of the year. The key to providing winter salads, then, is to have all plants well established by October to enable light cropping in the coming dark months. Plant too early and they try to run to flower before the dormant season; too late, and they remain tiny seedlings, sitting there helplessly as the blizzards descend. What this means is that, at this time of year, most of the leaves have to be replanted in one fell swoop rather than gradual succession; then we have to wait a month for them to get to harvesting size. This, my friends, is the *Salad Gap,* and we are slap bang in the middle of it.

This is not to say there are absolutely no leaves to be had: we've been scraping together a motley assortment to meet our regular commitments, but I can't pretend, as I normally do, that they represent a crafted blend of well-balanced flavours, textures and colour. So last week, with a cry of "let them eat tomatoes and cucumbers!", we sent no salad bags to the stall or box scheme.

There has been a small outcry over this, so we'll be sending salad gap bags to the stall this week, only I'd advise people to "cut" them with a head of lettuce, and perhaps a dressing sweetened with honey or maple syrup. By the end of September normal salad service should be resumed, with the host of delightful winter leaves – miners lettuce, corn salad, endive, chicory, baby kale, rucola rocket – to provide some sort of crisp consolation in the dying days.

Onto the Streets!

August 8, 2011

There's no stopping the stall: whatever the claims of supermarkets and internet shopping, every week millions clamour to rough-and-ready markets and car boot sales.

For over five years now, when Saturday comes we're selling and chatting by the busy roadside outside the Hornbeam Centre. It's a key "shopfront" for OrganicLea, and a key distribution outlet for Hawkwood produce and that of others: the *Cropshare* gardeners who bring their baskets of allotment surpluses from around the borough, and for Hughes Organics. The Hughes, Grahame and Lizzie, have an organic holding in Norfolk, and pool their veg with five other East Anglian growers to supply independent and community outlets in London. The stall, then, is weighed down and supported by food from alliances: rural/ urban; commercial/ subsistence. Recently we've started a second stall on the Leytonstone High Road, in alliance with Transition Leytonstone.

Market stalls certainly aren't as "efficient" a method of shifting our produce as box shemes and direct sales to restaurants, yet there is something spiritually and socially vital about *taking it to the streets*. The streets remain a vibrant democratic space of free activity and exchange: if we don't continuously claim this surviving commons, the privatising profiteers will.

Since June, we have also been at Walthamstow Farmers' Market once a month, where, due to the spirit and rules of true farmers' markets, we can only sell our own stuff. So the first week of each month I'm careful to hold back a decent volume and range of everything we have. On Thursday and Friday we're rewarded by a warehouse turned exotic with the rich blend of odours of twelve different living plants, exhaling and being trimmed.

Footballers talk of "setting out our stall" at the start of a game or a season: indeed, a prompt, purposeful display is what a good food market is all about. For us, this extends beyond the fresh items for sale, to include bountiful photos and flyers that tell the story of our attempt to create an alternative food system: "propaganda amongst the pumpkins", as we sometimes call it.

As the social dis-eases erupt into burning disturbances on the streets of north-east London this last couple of days, it's good to be out there[48], weather blowing from cold wind to blazing sunshine to showers, on Naomi and I, amongst the vegetables we've sown and grown: transplanted from the forest edge to Walthamstow High Street. It feels like what urban market gardening is all about.

Summer Break

August 18, 2011

Time was when I would look forward to a summer punctuated by a long cycling holiday: an aimless road trip over hills and dales; or carefree, car-free adventures in the Paradise region of France. Latterly, the demands and joys of the growing site have reduced such escapades to the odd day trip and TV coverage of the Tour de France. But this week I brought the garden and the cycling break together in doing our weekly delivery "into London Town".

Realising this year that we needed to look beyond our small beautiful box scheme and stall for homes for our urban market garden abundance, Clare, our intrepid Promotion and Distribution Worker, set out to find a few ideal partners. Idealists that we are, we weren't interested in flogging veg to any Tom, Dick or Harrods. We wanted people who were independent (for political and practical reasons: chainstores tend to bully small producers); we wanted people who rivalled our passion, shared our vision, and were ready to enter a long-term relationship. Ideally, they'd also be solvent, GSOH, and have a liking for late 80s indie pop, but there's only so much room in a lonely artichoke heart column.

Cutting to the happy ending, we found each other: Table 7 restaurant in Chingford, our lowest energy customer, courtesy of Ian's feet; Pizza East in Shoreditch, whom Deli Station, our Slow Food neighbours in the Lea Valley, deliver to on their capital rounds; and a convenient cluster of Camden cafés: The Sandwich Barge on the Regents Canal; Friends House on the Euston Road; Nice Green Van at the English Folk Song & Dance Society; and finally Manna, the "oldest vegetarian restaurant in London", purveyors of exquisite and ethical vegan cuisine.

For this "zero food miles" run, we focus on salad – a blend of leaves we're proud of and which has the advantage of being quite light – plus enough seasonal items to fill the trailer. The trailer is a Christiania, fabricated in the autonomous community of that name in Copenhagen, another practolitical choice: theirs is a car-free zone, so they've developed human-powered cargo carriers of utmost elegance and functionality.[49]

Empty polystyrene boxes are even lighter than salad, so there's a spring in my pedal as I leave Manna and journey east, retracing the historic cartwheels of so many growers and grocers. Squeezing through Islington traffic is not the same as spinning through fields and vineyards, it's true: but back then, I'd pass delightful vegetable patches and leave them behind. Now, I'm carrying them with me, at every turn.

Small Revolutions

August 26, 2011

I'm sure there's a deep-rooted human desire for full circles.

It's one of the fundamental pleasures of this work. It can be tough. Monday afternoon was set aside for pottering around nurturing the crops; instead, I became aware that the blight had made its unwelcome annual visit, and it was spent in a frenzy of scything, mowing down a field of potato foliage in time for the evening coop meeting, with only a grim satisfaction. Circles can be vicious, sure, but mostly they are restorative: the melons are ripe again, and the celery becomes ready.

Celery, as you may know, is a "cult classic" at Hawkwood Community Plant Nursery. This means it has a hardcore following and grows brilliantly here; so brilliantly that, last year, even the hardcore tired of seeing it in their vegeboxes, let alone the larger constituency of detractors. This year, a further plan was needed. Operation Shift Celery was born.

Growing Communities is a social enterprise in Hackney, which runs an organic box scheme, THE organic farmers' market, and urban market gardens supplying splendid salad to the former. Once upon a time I was a grower there: when push hoe came to shovel, I deemed that the next challenge for me personally, and the community food movement at large, was to develop broader-scale urban edge growing to back up the intensive pockets of production amongst the high dense. I vowed one day I'd return with a cartload of fringe vegetables.

When you leave something you love, promises of return some sunny day are a means of coping, hoping with the grief. Sometimes though, the wheel does run true.

This week we have had our second annual Soil Association inspection, which means we are officially "in organic conversion". And Growing Communities' buying policy allows for "in conversion" produce. Tuesday, for the first time, we picked, cleaned and packed in situ in the damp of the Entrance Field, the harvest being too big to haul through to the packing section of the warehouse. Nicole, an OrganicLea coop member and Growing Communities employee, fittingly masterminded the Operation.

As the drawing summer's evening drew in, Nicole and I pulled up at the Old Fire Station, GC's office and packing yard. There was some appreciation: this was their first delivery of "peri-urban" vegetables, a vital piece in their jigsaw of a community-controlled food system. A team of seven was packing the Hackney salad as we hauled out the Hawkwood specialities: the popular hit, our *Bull's Blood* beetroot, glowering crimson in the crates; and close to four hundred crisp clumps of a certain cult classic, virtually our whole bed's worth. Controversial celery: an ideal bring-back for a prodigal son.

A perfect circle.

Garlic Stores,
Onion Stories,
Tomato Restorations

August 20, 2012

"Everything dies, baby that's a fact / But maybe everything that dies / Someday comes back"
- Bruce Springsteen, "Atlantic City"

I love our garlic. Three years ago we tried the cultivar "Thermidrome" from the Rhone-Alpes region here, and from the unlikely origins of our thick London clay came forth full-flavoured cloves as fat as any I've seen grown organically in the UK. When it comes to vegetables, bigger is by no means better, but tiddly can certainly be fiddly.

Thermidrome has continued to yield well here, and when today our main seed merchant told me it was being discontinued, I sighed heavily, with what I hope they realised was a mixture of sadness and relief. The latter, because we have been keeping back a portion of the bulbs every year as insurance against discontinuations and other acts of God.

The garlic, once dried and cured in the glasshouse, wants storing in a cool, dry environment for the rest of its rest, from where, on rainy days and dark nights over the coming months, it will be cleaned, trimmed, hung, and steadily dropped into the Hawkwood farm stall and vegeboxes.

Last Wednesday seemed to be the ideal time to begin doing this: in the glasshouse they had stayed four weeks – a moon's circuit – a good period for the ripening of these clusters of pale crescents; and fiddling with unfiddly garlic was the best warm-up I could think of before a long weekend of traditional *cidre* and sun appreciation in northern France.

Cleaning up the fairest of our "seeds", my mind turned to the *Onion Johnnies*. Since the 1820s, these Breton farmers have crossed the windy channel with their cured onions, cousins of our French garlic. From there, they have ridden round the south of England – even as far as Wales if Dylan Thomas is to be trusted – pedalling their trade door to door, market place to market place. In doing so they sometimes died at sea; they gave us Brits the enduring stereotypical image of the Frenchman (hooped jersey, beret, moustache, garlands of plaited onions, roadster bicycles); and provide people like us with a colourful precedent for direct, human-powered produce.

In 1929 some 1,400 Johnnies imported over 9,000 tonnes of onions to Blighty, but by the end of the last century they had become a rare breed indeed. Yet their example inspired the founding of Brittany Ferries in the 1970s, primarily as a means of serving vegetables to the *rosbif*. The revived interest in real food has apparently led to a small revival in Johnny numbers trading their distinctive, protected varieties of pink Breton onions.

There is no "going back", and even if there was, there's quite probably no golden age to go back *to*. Yet if you see, as I do, our daily encounters with food and drink as one utterly fundamental encounter, or relationship if you will, with our world, then aftertastes of the past can bring meaning to that relationship, make it more meaning*ful*. Then the feats of the Onion Johnnies have a resonance when sorting Thermidrome garlic, some of which will be delivered by bicycle. Though not, I slightly regret, by men wearing waxed facial hair and berets.

I imagine the Breton farmer, their onions crispening in the summer heat, leaning on their sturdy three-speed, squinting over the blue body of water to locate the misty promise of the Hampshire coast.

From our Old Kitchen Garden you look out over the Lea Valley reservoirs, across the sea of houses to the fool's golden pavements of central London. In the days when Onion Johnny was in his pomp, fruit and veg markets were in the heart of the city, at Spitalfields and Covent Garden. No longer; but these sites continue to pulsate, with different trades layered over the still-visible seams of the produce exchange.

Then, market gardeners like us, on the skirts of London, ferried their harvests into these markets. It tickles me that, as of last week, we are in on the un-discontinuation of this tradition. The Opera Tavern, a tapas bar serving show-goers in Covent Garden (itself named after the nun's old kitchen garden that grew there before the veg market) is the most recent London eatery to stock our heritage tomatoes this summer. Welcome to the restoration.

Golden Detroit

August 5, 2013

"Calling out around the world, are you ready for a brand new beat?" - Martha & the Vandellas, *Dancing In The Street (1964)*

"Brothers and sisters, the time has come for each and every one of you to decide, whether you are gonna be the problem, or whether you are gonna be the solution." - MC5, *Kick Out The Jams (1969)*

Ours is a food growing garden, but nevertheless a garden, and I like to think that there are a few aesthetic touches the visiting ornamental gardener might appreciate. For instance, if you look down across the Entrance Field from just shy of Poets' Corner, you'll see plenty of flowers bursting amidst the vegetable foliage, and the odd nod to the "architectural" in the form of dappled sunflowers and tall Tuscan Kale. Peach trees embroider the glittering glasshouse walls in their tight-patterned fans; the green manure beds, now blooming in blues and mauves, have something of the Jekyllean herbaceous border about them come high summer; and the rows of annual crops spring up not in straight lines but sinuous curves hugging the contours, so that, in my more fanciful moments – and a bit of fancy is surely forgivable in August – I see the beetroot set out in its tricolour blocks as a kind of naturalistic potager.

The ever-dependable beets, like everything else at Hawkwood, emerge in a stable but always evolving range of cultivars. The tricolour consists of the deepest red – "Bull's Blood", or this year's trial "Cylindra", buttressed by the lighter "Barbietola di Chioggia" on the one flank and "Golden Detroit" on the other. Chioggia, also known as "candy beetroot" as its striking pink and white stripes resemble rock candy when sliced horizontally, comes of course from the town of Chioggia in Italy. The same place also gifted us "Marina di Chioggia" squash and "Catalogna Gigante di Chioggia" chicory. Such gastronomic generosity is not unusual in the Veneto province, a veritable hotbed of market gardening, where many of the vegetables now common or garden throughout Europe were initially bred and nurtured. It is to this region that I have been wistfully plotting a horticultural pilgrimage for some time, and I am looking forward to seeing Chioggia, a town apparently dominated by canals, much like Venice, or perhaps more exotically, Birmingham.

The strawberry blonde Golden Detroit is not just eye candy: flavourwise it is all high notes, without the tannic, earthy tones of traditional red varieties: a kind of summer cider to the Russian Stout of borscht. While Veneto may have a rich history of vegetable breeding in the round, when it comes to beetroot varieties Detroit, USA is some sort of epicentre. Alongside our Golden, we are growing "White Detroit" this year, and other seed catalogue regulars include "Detroit Crimson Globe"; "Detroit 2 Bolivar", "Perfected Detroit", "Detroit Dark Red Medium Top" and "Detroit-243". It seems these are all lines bred from the still-available "Detroit Dark Red", introduced in 1892 by the Motor City's PM Ferry Seed Company.

Sugar beet too has been grown extensively in the fields of Michigan State for many years, and is a close relative of table beet. So close that Christopher Stocks, in *Forgotten Fruits*, asks us to regard beetroot as a hero in the fight to abolish slavery, as beets were bred to offer a viable alternative source of sucrose to the cane plantations at the heart of the slave trade. Later, Detroit danced to different beats: Motown, the MC5 and the movements they soundtracked all lifting us closer to racial equality.

Nowadays, Detroit is that rare phenomenon: a shrinking city. Since the decline of the car industry, the population has dropped from 1.8 million to 700,000. This poses all kinds of problems for those remaining, but also some opportunities. Many residents have taken to growing food in the empty "lots", organically sprouting an estimated two thousand productive gardens. Town planners have had to embrace the space, and have drawn up plans for "blue-green corridors" through the city. It may be not so fanciful to see in Detroit the possibility that, from the crises of capitalism, might emerge healthy, sustainable eco-cities. In which case discs of beautiful beetroot, whatever their colour, will once again play a bit part in progressive social change.[50]

Pick of the Pickles

August 20, 2013

I've just returned from my summer travels. I say this matter-of-factly, yet it has been some ten years since I took a week's break during this, the height of the season. But so proficient have the Hawkwood team and its "Plants & Production" nucleus of Gary, Vi, Aimée, Jonny, Mary and Hannah become, that I have quite run out of excuses for loitering around the garden all summer becoming a bit of a nuisance. Adam, along with former apprentice Asia and Hannah Leigh Mackie (of Growing Communities and Stepney City Farm notoriety) stepped in charitably, to take me on a pilgrimage... ... Or *picklegrimage*, as we quickly dubbed it. The mission was simple yet daring: a visit to the Podlaskie region of Poland, taking tasting notes on the array of ways in which various vegetables are traditionally preserved in the "Wild East". I imagine if I was a plumber, and themed my holidays around the study of, say, Andorran elbow joints, friends and family would pull me aside for a few stern but fair words in my shell-like. Somehow, though, I'm allowed to get away with these vegetable-driven capers.

Thus, in the absence of any such rational advice, we cycled and grazed our way through many manifestations of stilled cabbage, onion, patty pan, courgette, mushroom, shallot, carrot, pepper, garlic, chilli, beetroot; and of course Ogorke, the gherkin: Poland's premier pickle. True gherkins in fact remain largely the preserve of African and Caribbean cuisine, while the European versions are almost always pickled small-ridge cucumbers. Not that this worried us: too immersed were we in debates as to the ideal balance between sweet, sour and salty; crunchy and juicy; vinegar versus lacto-fermentation; the relative virtues of fresh "fizzy" and mellow aged versions; and the range of herbs and spices to aid the process and add the necessary bite.

The vitality of the pickling culture was evidenced in the shops, stalls, dining tables, and, naturally, in the fields and gardens. In the latter, cucumbers, dill and horseradish were as ubiquitous as staple potatoes. In the former, carved into the ubiquitous potatoes and the blue-to-green herds of cabbage, stood slices of garden: handmade and mixed planted. As in other areas of Europe with more equitable land distribution than ours, the twine between allotment and farm, between peasant and commercial production, holds.

With the notable exceptions of our apple pressing and annual Green Tomato Chutney Day, produce leaves Hawkwood ultra-fresh, rather than processed in any way, so learning from the picklegrimage will be applied in the domestic sphere, and join the raft of future project dreams.

More immediately, I return to sunflowers that have put on a few feet in my absence, green peppers that have jumped red, and cucumbers in a totally new light. We eschew the "glasshouse" types so beloved of our Upper Lea Valley neighbours: they're too straight, a bit bland and, I'll be honest, a bit difficult to grow. Instead, we go for the rugged and flavoursome: "Marketmore", a fat English ridge standard that would look perfectly at home in a Polish country garden or pickle jar; and the slender reptilian "Soyu Long" that, by contrast, sticks out a mile. They do however taste great and remind us that cue culture extends way beyond our landmass. And no one has yet contested Aimée's hypothesis that this cultivar is the actual "snozzcumber" cited in Roald Dahl's *BFG*.

Red spider mite also has a particular penchant for cucumbers, and this tiny insect was taking its toll on many of the Podlaskie plants. At Hawkwood, it's the one thing that hasn't moved much: the growers here have clearly been conscientiously damping down to slow its spread. It's to these efforts I'll rejoin. And, knowing that the crop has a month's swan song before giving way to the winter brassicas, and in the absence of major pickling operations, I'll seek, in the mind's brine, other sure ways of savouring the glow of these great green gods.

September

Happy Endings

September 15, 2010

Keats had it that autumn is the "season of mists and mellow fruitfulness", but the growers' tour of fruity duty extends from the solstice to the frosts, with now, late summer, at its most fulsome. Here at Hawkwood, the balance of power began to shift from the leaves to the fruit just after the longest day: the fruiting *vegetables*, that is. For, botanically speaking, fruits are seed-associated structures; horticulturally and culinarily speaking, vegetables are any plant eaten fresh in savoury dishes. So our first fruits were June's indoor French beans, followed by the outdoor French beans, the rich and varied tomatoes in late July, and now the onset of peppers, hot and sweet, a living legacy of summer.

The summer squash "Vegetable Spaghetti" is an esoteric specimen, inspiring devotion from its small band of followers and puzzlement from everyone else. We've been steadily bringing in the winter squash for the last month, and gave the "Green Hokkaido" a satisfactory test ride at the Permaculture Design Course at the weekend but these, like the winter brassicas, won't be on general release until the air starts to smell of autumn proper, triggering that simple twist of palate from the "lighter" foodstuffs to the dense comforts of roots, tubers and stored *fruits*.

But it is the squashes' cousins indoors that we pay tribute to at these times. Earlier on this year, as you will recall if you scroll back, there were all sorts of traumas associated with the *Cucurbitaceae* bed in the glasshouse. But this story at least has a happy ending: the cucumbers, late-sown replacements, have been prolific. So much so that in the face of my ruthless pragmatism when it comes to such matters I felt on the verge of raising a toast and making a speech in their honour as we pulled them up, still proffering gherkin-sized young, last Tuesday, to make way for the impatient winter rocket.

Divorced from their stalks, the last cucumber fruits were piled into crates with no particular place to go. It was Clare's plan to take them to the Saturday stall and initiate a special Eid discount cucumber offer. This saw our weekly sales of the cool green things rocket from 10 to 70, and perhaps launched a brand new tradition.

Then there's the melons. Thirty months of hurt never stopped me dreaming. For two years in a row, my team and I have tended these tender plants but failed to reap a ripe dessert. They're tricky but they seem worth it: they have the yum!/ wow!/ snack! factor that means they – especially if they're local and organic – fly off the proverbial shelves in a way that, say, celery and Jerusalem artichokes, frankly, don't.

Our melons are a tabloid gardening columnist's dream: once victims of the Woodlice Fiasco Horror Shambles, they are now Bra-Busting Essex Beauties, after our realisation that second-hand underwear was an ideal supporting structure for them. This week, we picked. They are less sweet, but deeper flavoured, than their European counterparts, although that's all academic: the point is, they are bloody *melons*, and we grew 'em, and have eaten them. And you can never take that away from us.

I'm often amazed at how even novice gardeners can be so hopeful/ over-ambitious when it comes to growing things that are at the limit of their range: outdoor tomatoes are a classic example; and on a visit this week to the brilliant Grow Heathrow[51], in their first year of renovating a derelict market garden on the site of the shelved Third Runway, aubergine plants were more conspicuous than courgettes.

I prefer to stick with the tried and tested in the garden – well, at least 80 per cent of the time. But there's something about the novelty, the risky and the challenging. Perhaps it's that 20 per cent of new, risky challenges that keep us doing the rest, that keep us gardening, doing sports, loving, that keep us alive. Hooray for melons.

Blight on the Landscape

September 26, 2010

At first glance, it might seem that vegetable growing serves as a detachment from the grand narratives of humanity, compared with, say, commuting through London's labyrinth of iconic streets, or working as a new part amongst the original engines of industrialisation: mills, mines or railways. In fact, plant biographies chronicle social history as well as any architecture or museum, and what's more, they are living and breathing.

Last week I was in the Entrance Field mowing green manures. Perched above the clover sat the plump beetroot, who contributed to the abolition of slavery when Europeans found they could process them into sucrose, thus reducing the dependency on slave-dependent cane sugar. Down the hill stood the evergreen cabbages and kales, which have served us well as the "paupers' medicine" for millennia, from the pickled cabbage of the Far East across to the "kale yards" of the Scottish crofters. My blade sliced through clover, that fertility-building legume which formed the cornerstone of "Turnip" Townsend's rotation, a prerequisite of the "Agricultural Revolution". It is on clover and its Fabaceae relatives that hopes for abundance in a post-oil future rest heavily.

And towering above these fresh mowings in the adjacent bed was the larger-than-life *Solanum tuberosum*: the potato; the Andean tuber that revolutionised diet and culture in Europe and beyond.

Spuds are, economically, the most important vegetable in the world, and the third most important plant crop. Their virtues are many, but in leaner times impoverished peoples in temperate climates turned to them chiefly because: a) they are a complete food, containing all the major and minor nutrients in sufficient quantities to sustain human existence (bar the elusive vitamin B12); and b) they produce more calorific energy per given area than any other crop.

Thus, for example, the Irish people, forced onto marginal land by the British colonists, were able to survive (or, perhaps, were able to be further exploited) thanks to their total conversion to the "earth apple". Which brings us, terribly neatly, to what else I saw whilst scything: *Phytophthora infestans*, the dreaded potato blight. It's a very small fungus, but can also lay claim to changing the course of global events; for it caused the Irish Potato Famine, 1845–47, and subsequent emigration of the Irish peoples across the Anglophone world.

Catching the blight early enough to save the spuds is, like so much, all about observation: this year I was slow off the mark, and whether we've stopped the disease reaching the tubers remains to be seen. It is an ugly mould that will cause some nervousness in these parts over the next few weeks. But this is as nothing when set against the plight of those Irish peasants, whose shadow loomed large as we went about our blight management work. During which I reflected on how the disease was brought to Europe in a crate of infected potatoes from the Americas, and how once great blight-resistant cultivars like "Lady Eve Balfour" are now succumbing to it, as new strains of the fungus are moved efficiently around the world – in another symptom of the sicknesses caused by excessive global food and plant supply chains. But that's another story, perhaps one day another history.

Corn Again

September 6, 2011

We've just had our annual "Design Fusion" event, where the Hawkwood core team look at the growing site and set priorities for developments over the coming year. As is the tradition, the process began with a "visioning" exercise, where we each imagined the Nursery in five years' time. When the utopian visions were relayed, it was striking that only one vegetable was specifically singled out for mention, not once, but twice. That vegetable was sweetcorn. For a relatively minor and recent addition to our planting plan, this was no mean achievement.

I could offer a few explanations as to why *Zea mays* is "straight in at number one" amongst the growers here at Hawkwood. They're an impact plant: as you enter Free London through the Community Nursery gates, they raise their fists to you from the Entrance Field, rising up above the low-lying vegetables. At over six foot, we sense that, somewhere in our primordial souls, our spirits seek a vertical range in the landscape, a dimension sadly lacking in most annual crops.

For me, corn will forever echo the Mayan *milpa* plantings I witnessed in January, incredibly gardened in sheer scree in the mountains of Chiapas. *Lento pero avanzo* (slowly, but we advance) — as the "people of the maize", the Zapatista indigenous communities, say.

Maybe it's this local growing of a global plant that we like: at the Hornbeam Café Ryan, a great advocate of food as a bridge across cultures, was allegedly moved to tears on experiencing "Caribbean" corn coming down from Chingford; while a couple of weeks ago I was in the field when an African man pulled up in his car, got his child out of the back, walked up to the towering plant and proceeded to demonstrate, in energetic gesticulations, how corn on the cob is borne.

Maybe these are reasons why we want to see this golden grain growing more prolifically here into the future. But somehow I feel these are all secondary: the crux of the matter is that corn on the cob, with a smattering of butter or oil, and salt or pepper if you will, is up there with the best of all culinary experiences. And, like asparagus, globe artichokes and strawberries, its season — its true, local season — is so short, so sweet.

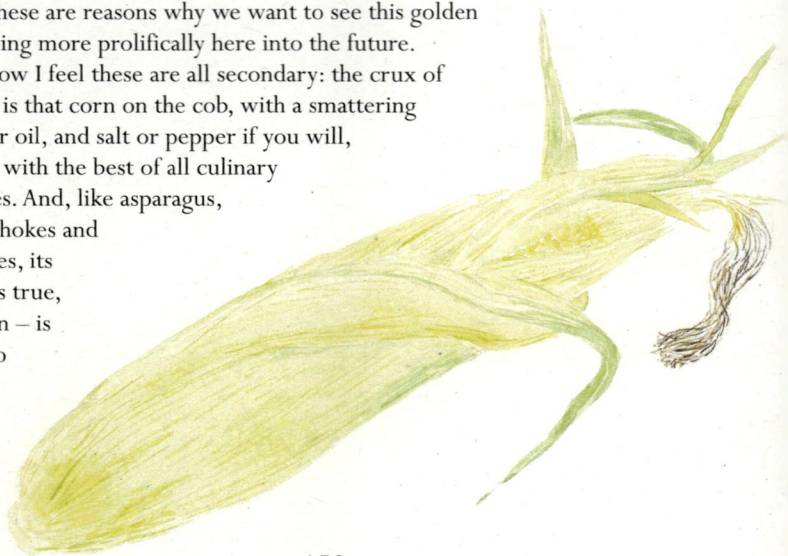

Interesting Times

September 14, 2011

When talking of his formative years, through the second world war, my grandfather
– the one-time tomato farmer – likes to quote Dickens: "they were the best of times,
and the worst of times". The Chinese proverb throws yin-yang light on the matter:
"may you live in interesting times".

These are interesting times. We are hurtling into an age of "climate chaos", huge
environmental and social upheavals. One *hope* is that the worst of climate change will
be arrested by *peak oil,* the not-unsettling prospect of the fossils that fuel our economy
running low. And yet, these are great days we're living in right now: autumn's golden
aura crowds our peripheral; while in our brighter moments we are Indian summer.
As above, so below: the pumpkin leaves are withering to reveal the fiery glow of the
"Uchiki Kuri" squash; the chicory leaves turn green to red with each colder bite of
night.

Walking Tractor Attachment Of The Month this September is the Potato Lifter. In
the Old Kitchen Garden, Sean and I, with cameo appearances from apprentices Jo
and Naomi, creep up front, manhandling four horsepower to unfold the ridges of *Isle
of Jura,* while a fairly chirpy gang follows in the furrows, gathering vegetable gold in
hessian sacks, grading out the holey and blighty.

It's just like the tattie harvest as described to me by one lady brought up in
1950s Ireland. And it's what a sensible "low-carbon" future will look like: oil-
powered machinery summoned up for occasional, high-impact jobs, while the more
sophisticated tools – human hands and eyes – are relied on for the finer detail. The
oil our tractors run off is recycled chip fat. On combustion, the exhaust fumes do
indeed smell of chip shops: a most auspicious incense to accompany the sacred potato
picking ritual.

A few bright leaves drop on us as we cart our heavy haul into the warehouse,
passing Nicole and her team manually pressing "scrumped" apples into juice, and for
cider vinegar.

In the good times; in the bad times; in the interesting times: there will be chips and
vinegar.

Autumn Leaves

September 28, 2011

So much seasonal excitement that it's easy to take some things, like your heart and your breath, for granted. That's what this time is for: Autumn Equinox. Harvest-tide. A time of thanksgiving for the many wonderful people and plants who have appeared at the nursery and given their all. This equinox, I choose a perch above the West Bank Salad Terrace as my "sit spot" to reflect on the fading growing season.

It's not the most picturesque location. Tucked at the lower end of the site, it doesn't command the sweeping forest and cityscape views of the vineyard or *Poets' Corner* above the Entrance Field. There's still a lot of dirty black plastic keeping the horsetail down. And the concrete paths that define the terraces, a legacy of the council bedding bays, lend the space a harder, more artificial flavour than the curving swards of the Orchard or Old Kitchen Garden.

But it's those same cement slabs and level terra firma that made the West Bank the obvious choice for intensively-managed, garden-scale, raised beds of leaves.

Here, on Tuesday mornings, come rain – or, more often – shine, you will find many of the aforementioned wonderful people, carrying out all the planting, weeding, picking and troubleshooting that goes into our signature product – mixed salad leaves.

This year, our mix has featured 37 different leaves, 48 different plant cultivars, and seven different edible flowers. Not all have been triumphs, and still, more often than not, the blend or the quality is imperfect. But no excuses or complaints: I can't imagine a better growing season for salad.

That hot, dry April and May brought out glorious swansongs in the winter lettuce and rocket, while getting the spring-sown freshers to maturity quickly and slug-free. Then, in the ensuing warmth and moisture, they just got on with it. The shade cloths and seep hose were barely called into action: all the hard graft Huf, Ed and Sonny put into overhauling the irrigation system was repaid elsewhere: under glass, and on thirsty apple maidens.

We'll be getting salad off the terraces and, even at sub-zero, out of the glasshouse, almost every week of the year. So, as we ponder the dark times ahead, we can console ourselves with the thought that the young chicories, mizunas, endives, winter purslanes, et al, will be a constant source of freshness through the winter; a bridge between the lost summer and the distant horizon of spring; colour in the absence of broadleaves and flowers.

Cold snaps will make their texture tougher, but will also convert some of their starches into sugars. Autumn and winter: I'll take them hard, sweet, dependable, and be thankful.

Fire Power

September 2, 2012

Though the Indian summer, or its mirage, stretches to the horizon, still the world has tilted us into autumn. The light is decidedly shorter and lower, and its emotional quality is altered. And radicchio doesn't lie: like litmus it tints deeper in direct proportion to the deepening night temperatures. Right now on the Entrance Field these chicory leaves are torn between summer green and the scarlet shades that give "Orchidea Rossa", "Rossa di Treviso" and "Grumolo Rossa" their names.

In the garden, the tide has changed. Adam – our Mister Versatile, having played in every position this season, from Apprentice grower to box scheme logistics to Network Development worker – put it well this week when he said "it's too late to do anything now". Anything, that is, but look, exhale, weed. Things are now growing by themselves, or not at all. The summer crops cannot be induced to grow more, nor replanted if they don't. It's time to delight in the joys and admit the defeats: after weeks of carefully pruning blighted potato foliage, now we cut it to the ground, cut our losses; the twice re-sown, slug-ridden French bean bed will give us one bean if that: we can only look forward to healthy field beans in the not-too-distant; on the bright side, we have fabulous beetroot, tomatoes, and, just lately, chilli peppers.

What better plant to carry the flame of the summer into the cold dark days? In spring the glasshouse is full of seedlings, for us and for plant sales, but when these fly to greener pastures, the sand-lined staging becomes Hot Pepper Beach, swarming with sunbathing containerised capsicums. It seems to be a happy timeshare arrangement: they fruit OK in pots.

As resorts go, it's pretty international: we have "Bolivian Rainbow", a multicoloured specimen I picked up in Andalucia at the start of the year; "Serrano", "Habanero" and "Jalapeno" from the chilli cultural capital Mexico; Scotch Bonnet "Safi" from the Caribbean; "Soverato" from farmers resisting land expropriation in the Susa Valley, Italy; Jim's Long Cayenne from Australia; and the Yankee "Ring of Fire". And going into the vegeboxes last week were the mild, large, orange-red torpedoes of "Hungarian Hot Wax".

Ah, the magnificent Magyars. Hungary is the first, arguably the only, European culture to welcome the chilli plant and make it their own, so much so that *Paprika*, as they know it, is their national cuisine's totem. How this came to be is disputed: the Turks are widely credited with introducing it when they ruled Hungary as part of the Ottoman Empire in the sixteenth and seventeenth century.

However, an indigenous folktale turns that story on its head. Once, a beautiful Hungarian girl was out walking in the fields near where she lived, which was close to a Turkish barracks. She was abducted and imprisoned in the local harem. The Turks, like the Mayans before them, knew of the pepper's aphrodisiac qualities, so they spiked their food and that of the harem girls with chillies of the paprika variety. The girl desperately missed her freedom, and her boyfriend, and one day discovered a secret passage to the outside world. She escaped, was reunited with her lover, but had to return to the harem to avoid punishment. Before doing so, she slipped him some capsicum seeds she had pocketed inside. Soon after, pepper plants started growing all over the countryside. The resistance fighters were fortified and fired up by their new spicy diet, so much so that they fought the Turks out of the territory.

Whether this is how it happened or not, this myth tells of an important historical process: that of the oppressed taking something of the oppressor's, and turning it against them. Like the use of liberal and Christian ideas in struggles against racism and colonialism; or using social media to question and expose global capitalism. There is a further salutary lesson in it: while we suffer daily for the greed of a few millionaires, we need only see that we can all be, as Mary here would say, *chillionaires*. Time to get fired up!

Gardening Leave

September 14, 2012

The *community* market garden offers the grower the possibility of tearing themselves away during the main season, safe in the knowledge that the collective will keep things tended. It's a variation on the support structures that are natural in "traditional" farming communities. In Chiapas, every farmer does a month long *stint* in the militia, defending the autonomous Zapatista villages from state and para-state attacks, trusting their neighbours to take care of their land. In Tuscany, Italy, people in the same area continue the tradition of getting together to assist each other with the grape *vendemmia* (harvest) and the *raccolta* (collection) of olives.

This is where I've been, not to help with either event, but to help myself to wayside figs and herbs, and to any spillings of wisdom I can glean from Tuscan horticultural and culinary culture.

The "happy serendipity", as Colin Tudge calls it, is that the best food in the world is the most nutritious, and the most ecological. This is peasant food: plant-based, crafted with passion from the grain of the environment and climate. In Tuscany, the peasant fare triangulates with stunning landscape and ancient history: a holy trinity that so many tourist pilgrimages seek to touch and be touched by.

Within this holy trinity is another: the grape, the olive and the wheat: the ancestors of Tuscan life and the building blocks of their world-famous *cuisine*. The former two have been cultivated in the Mediterranean for 8,000 years, and carry that weight of ancestral memory. As do the indigenous herbs – rosemary, marjoram, thyme. More recent introductions, such as garlic, basil, tomatoes, zucchini, have received subsequent sanctification. In a place where food is accurately regarded as the source of life, somehow sacred: these are vegetable gods.

This plant mysticism still has roots because it remains *of the people*. With the partial exception of wheat, they are all prepared fresh from garden plants. The key vegetables are grown in back gardens and farm corners; along with vines and olives which, though grown on plantation-scale, also have their local mills and presses for production that is small-scale, or, as they say, "misura d'umo" – to the measure of humans.

All this doesn't necessarily make Tuscany a better place, a better society: only in some ways. At the least, it should compel any self-respecting British citizen returning from a jolly out there to consider what they are bringing to, and taking from, the shrine at this Harvest Festival time.

Plants such as cabbage, parsnips, celery and broad beans go back to the earliest of gardens on these isles, yet are sometimes regarded with disdain rather than reverence. Earlier still, gatherings of green leaves – saladings – would have played a vital role in the diet of the first Britons, and some of the contents of our mixed salad bags, such as burnet, sorrel, watercress, mint, chard – would have been instantly recognisable to them. Later generations of Britons have brought tomatoes, runner beans, corn, okra, gourds, transplanting a crop menu as rich and intricate in its breadth as traditional peasant societies are in their depth.

The cornerstones of the UK diet, namely the grains, are now the preserve of highly mechanised farms. But there is a *hum*an-scale exception: the *hum*ble potato. The tuber is a complete food, easily grown, preserved and prepared at home and in the community. From chips to saag aloo, mash to colcannon, roasties to gnocchi: these hidden treasures run a seam through so much of the rich UK food tapestry today.

Back at Hawkwood, it is three weeks since we cut back the blighted foliage, and a dozen or so people will this week come together to do their *stint* (literally: the term originated with potato pickers) in the Entrance Field and the packhouse.

As we're picking in the Field, we'll look across at the kales, the closest relatives of our indigenous wild cabbage: "Pentland Brigg", a stalwart of Scottish crofters; and the latterly popular "Nero di Toscano" – Tuscan Black. Above the wise old celery are saladings of chicory and Lolla Rossa, and the golden jewels of pumpkin flowers still unfolding. Our Italian-inspired friends at Table 7 Bistro love these delicacies, but I'm still not sure what to do with them. Maybe I'll make that a Late Summer Resolution. Maybe someone here has an idea. Maybe *la dolce vita* isn't so far from this burnt, oily valley as it might at first glance seem.

Changing of the Gourds

September 25, 2012

"We are changing the rhythms of nature by which we have lived our lives and planted our crops and written our poetry for the last 10,000 years."- B. McKibben

In this age of carbonated climate insecurity, all the more tear jerking the joy when the seasons turn to show a recognisable face. We *did* have a summer after all, late and glorious *for a' that*. Yields per acreage are down, but not out, in many areas; in some they have held: nature is, as ever, more forgiving and generous than we have the right to expect. The beetroot and tomatoes have been fantastic in every way, and the high-rise sweetcorn has ripened, which didn't seem highly likely a couple of months ago.

The golden cobs are, as we speak, being enthusiastically endorsed by Epping Forest's grey squirrel population. This is not the result of any nature-inspired unexpected generosity on our part, only of our inferior wit. The tussle between human and rodent intelligences is one of gardening's timeless spectacles. It is, variously, endlessly fascinating or rather tiresome, depending, frankly, on whether we're winning or not. The rats have been driven out of the glasshouse, but this year the squirrels have won the Hundred Maize War. Fortunately, growing veg is, as Bradley Wiggins said of the Tour de France, "not the World Cup: it comes around every year". Next season, there'll be all to play for, and we hope to have the Jolly Green Giant on our side.

More joyfully, the shift from summer to autumn happened bang on the equinox, ancient textbook fashion, a cold wet front arriving just as night drew level with day. And this week, the changing of the gourds. A seamless Hawkwood relay.

This is us at our best: Adam picked the last of the "Suyo Long" cucumbers on Tuesday afternoon. Mary's team cleared to compost their wrinkly plant remains on Wednesday morning, and after lunch Dean and Steven planted brassica salads in their wake. These snake-like cucumbers have been our rising stars: they come with a flavour subtle and surprisingly sweet, in a range of comical shapes and sizes. Slow food restaurants and farm stall customers have preferred them to our mainstay "ridge" type. The variety's trump card, though, is that it is one of a precious few vegetables that you can not only eat, but also drink (in Pimm's) and wear (as scarves, necklaces, bracelets). Build a shelter out of them and that's all your basic needs sorted.

As the last of these versatile reptiles lies coiled on the farm stall, I see Dean stand back from its compatriot replacement, Oriental Mustard, and Ed passes by carrying the first of another Eastern-East End delight, a crate of "Uchiki Kuri" pumpkin, freshly picked from the Entrance Field. It dawns on me that there could be few more fitting events to mark the autumn equinox: the cucumber, which gives us moon-like discs of liquid cool to balance thirsty summers, is eclipsed by its cucurbit sister, the fiery red squash, whose bright globes warm our hearts and bellies into the winter.

The earth has turned. For one more year, we can live our lives, plant our crops, write our poetry. Amen.

Not One to Wine

September 6, 2013

It's difficult to overstate the English capacity to not overstate things. When asked how we are, or what the weather's been like, responses may range dramatically from "alright", through "bearing up", all the way to "can't complain". You could say it reflects a moderate – even fatalistic – streak, which, like all cultural traits, can be charming at times and at others infuriating; though we mustn't grumble, I suppose. It's this *sweet moderation* that has, on the one hand, put the damper on historical movements that brought us to within grasping reach of liberation, and on the other, stemmed autocratic tyranny to a degree. Ultimately, like all traditions, at important moments it is there to be thrown out. Now is one such: this growing season has been neither "OK" nor "not too bad"; neither "quite good" nor "better than a slap in the face": it has been gob-smackingly, jaw-droppingly EXCELLENT.

Except for the slow start, we couldn't have asked for more: warm, good light levels, regular, deep rainfall. Growth has been lush yet balanced, inside and out. No pest or disease has run rife, and the biggest problem we've faced is working out just what, apart from the obscene, to do with all those cucumbers and celery sticks. This is, as they say "a nice problem to have". (The solution for the latter item has been, bizarrely, to sell them to organic box scheme operators in Norfolk and Devon. This certainly wasn't the objective when we set up a food growing project in London, though it might represent some sort of a landmark in the development of urban production here!)

The dreaded late-summer Salad Gap barely appeared; the winter leaves just gushed forth to replace the tired spring sown ones, with time to spare. The job is now to discourage premature flowering. The tomatoes, odd spates of blossom end rot and splitting aside, have been truly, madly, deeply superb. The Old Kitchen Garden is awash with squash. And the Entrance Field stands tall, and clean: we are on top of the weeds as never before. Resting on laurels is never wise, especially not in the garden, but equally it'd be rude not to stand back and breathe the sweet, earthy smell of success, on behalf of all of those who have laboured to get the garden to this praiseworthy point.

With our horticultural training still in the holidays, and the crops mature and managed, the more intense energy on site at the moment – where the race is still being run – is around the harvesting. Joining the thick vegetable scoop are the fruits: raspberries and cape gooseberries; while our Scrumping Project once again welcomes would-be-wasted household apples and pears. Meanwhile Marko and the vineyard team are putting the

finishing touches to the winery just as the grapes get ready to glow.

The winery, our fairly obvious solution to the problem of just what to do with all the grapes, has already fermented into something a bit richer. Country wine is already on the menu, a surprising weight of free range bramble fruit being plucked from hitherto largely disregarded scrub and shrubs of our biodiversity areas. And we've launched the community wine-making scheme. Through this, Londoners who have grapes growing in their garden, by happenstance or design, will merge their yields into one great, multi-varietal vintage (or rather, one red one white). More than celery to Devon, this marks the next small step for our alternative food system. All over the world, small producers come together to pool resources, be it in the form of grain mills, combine harvesters or marketing cooperatives: this tradition of mutual aid is a hallmark of peasant societies.

Time and again the experts of Right and Left have pronounced the death of the peasant mode of production. Yet it lives: it not only, as Patrick Mulvaney of UK Food Group points out, continues to feed the majority of the world's people[52], it also re-emerges in late capitalist societies such as ours, in the form of community wine making schemes, allotments, and urban market gardens. It keeps coming back, like the seasons. Like this gorgeous late summer sun; like the red of the radicchio; like that ripe hint at autumn.

Sarvari Potato More

September 24, 2013

Friday the thirteenth's "Harvest of Stories" felt a fitting way to round off the summer. A public feast in the glasshouse, where it was exactly warm enough to sit for an evening. Although the changes had been rung on some of the beds, where mere glints of winter salad plants are making the first small grips into their incredible journey, all the climbing crops still stood tall and resplendent: in the candlelight they surely merged into deep curtains drawing into the night.

The stories, told by different voices, pertained to the different plant species and varieties grown at Hawkwood, now transformed into the fantastic feast. Some of these tales have been touched in previous Musings: others await their opening into these particular pages. The story of the potato, from Raleigh's alleged introduction to the Great Hunger, leaves a shadow longer than most plants in our taught history. Marlene recounted a further chapter:

On the very evening that a full "Smith period" blight warning was declared in our E4 area, we were reminded of the work of Dr. Sarvari, a Hungarian who began breeding potatoes for high blight resistance and achieved some success. Potato blight is a dynamic, mutating disease. While "conventional" famers can respond to this quality with repeated sprays – last year many will have applied copper-based fungicides up to twenty times – the organic grower eschews the long-term damage this causes, relying entirely on cultural methods, a key one being resistant varieties. Yet so shape-shifting is the Phytophthora fungus that firm immune favourites such as Lady Eve Balfour have now become susceptible. Enter the Sarvari Trust.

Dr. Sarvari took his findings to Scottish and Danish potato growers, and a Trust has been established in Wales, developing the "Sarpo" range of potatoes to the point of commercial availability. The Sarpos are by all accounts, at present at least, extraordinarily dismissive of the crippling sickness. In the Entrance Field, the dense green foliage of our Sarpo Mira hasn't flinched as the wind and rain toss fungal spores this way and that; while under the protection of glass our tomatoes steadily succumb. As we face a period of increasingly uncertain weather conditions, the Sarvari Trust are one of the Great White Hopes for sustainable spuds.

Last year, the unfunded Trust raised £10,000 through crowd fundraising to continue its research. Meanwhile, over in Norwich, the John Innes Centre Sainsbury Laboratory have secretively, unaccountably, spent £1.7 million of public money failing to develop a genetically modified, blight-resistant potato. Last year campaigners from Britain and beyond, including a delegation from London's Community Food Growers' Network, visited the laboratory to tell them and the government the good news: we've found the potato you're looking for! This year, their trials continue apace.

It's not unusual, the sacrificing of commons sense on the altar of corporate profit, but examples such as this throw the matter into sharp relief. There was sharp relief also on the day of the banquet, when Paul and Ed dug up the first few tubers. Last year, the day of the great Potato Lift yielded but a few rotten, infested remnants; this year, a return to that primordial pleasure of finding Irish gold, "loving the cool hardness in our hands", as the just-late Seamus Heaney put it[53].

Sarpo Mira, it has to be said, doesn't boast the wonderful flavour of a Pentland or the Arran Victory: they are not a panacea; the quest continues for the holy grail of the potato, or indeed any vegetable cultivar, which marries radiant health with superb flavour and impressive yields. But at least in three weeks, when we bring in the maincrops, we will have *plenty* in our winter store. They will each tell tales of summer sun, when roasted in months to come; of decent, honest human labour and enquiry; of working with, not against, nature, and all the full promises that brings.

A Question of Time

September 29, 2013

"Horticulture is the last refuge of the unemployable": this quote from James Sinclair was brought to my attention recently by the grower Sam Eglington. A quip it may have been, but a glance at the CVs, and shevelment status, of those labouring at Hawkwood reveal it to be almost a profound truth.

The paid coop members here are a motley crew of dropouts, transplanted PANSiEs[54], rat race retirees and odd-jobbers. Most of us were happily playing with our food, until we somehow got stuck on the payroll. This gives us a slightly stunned demeanour, reminiscent of a seventeen year old suddenly put out to perform at Wembley, by which we can be told apart from the volunteers. Of this latter group, who span the whole spectrum of "Employment Status": a third "work full time", or have a proper job, in old money, thus lending the project some air of respectability.

That is, up until now. This week, Hawkwood Community Plant Nursery is a featured garden on Radio 4's Gardeners' Question Time. This is the longest running gardening broadcast in the world, and one of the few horticultural institutions established enough to legitimately drop the "horti" bit. For some time now we will be able to bask in its reflected acceptability, a fact only amplified by our mention, on Monday, in that boss class rag, the *Financial Times*.

We won't be the only ones basking in this Indian summer light. Last week we marked the autumn equinox, that great turning point, in the way we know how: bringing the prodigal squash suns home, from the wild fields to the cosseted glasshouse where their life's journey began.

It was a big, dramatic, nervy, logistical operation. The challenge: to get the maximum number of proficient pumpkin pickers out; bringing in all, and only, the mature specimens; with minimum damage to fruit, plants and soil; with as much anarchy and as little chaos as possible; in the four hours of official Work Day available.

In many ways, it was the mirror image of the Great Squash Planting Out. This occurred on a drizzly late-May day, at the end of which we looked back at the little plants, set out with their tall order to fill the large dark space of the Old Kitchen Garden. The satisfaction with which we turned away that day has returned, only the accompanying anxiety replaced with joy.

The squashes, all nine spread-eagling varieties of them, are our biggest crop this year in every sense: covering the biggest land area (the whole Old Kitchen Garden, four beds of the Entrance Field and their trialled two rows of the Vineyard), weighing in at up to fourteen kilos each, and now covering a sizeable portion of the glasshouse's hard landscape. They've filled their allotted space, and some: the original harvest date had to be postponed for a fortnight, until the leaves furled enough to allow us to see, and see our way to, the hidden orange/ yellow/ green/ blue/ brown/ red treasure.

As with the planting, we settled on the classic Pairs formation for the picking team, each unit making their own tendril-like songlines through the dense dance of the pumpkin patch. Squash superstars like Paul, Ed, Gary and Aimée played pivotal roles in this final reckoning, having gone the full circle from seed to feed to weed to reward, while more recent arrivals like Jess and Margo showed impressive strength in lifting the heavyweight trophies.

The number of people who participated in, and have come to marvel at, the squash harvest at Hawkwood, makes a mockery of the recited dogma that "people don't want to work the land anymore". People don't want lives of drudgery and poverty, but working the land no more has to be that than does being a professional athlete, a computer programmer, or a postie: it's just how our weird world has ordered it. So it can be re-ordered, little by little, step by step, bottom to top. "It goes on one at a time/ it starts when you care to act", says Marge Piercy in "The Low Road". Later, there will be pumpkin pie.

And I am proud of what we have here, the people, the land, and the riotous gathering of gourds that make the harvest festival display in the glasshouse. After the difficult growing season last year, they sum up this summer. Over a thousand strong, fully ripe, grown to organic standards and of good eating quality. For a little London garden: pretty respectable.

About the Size of it

September 2, 2014

We seem to be coming to an end: leaves are turning to glow in the cucumber cool of morning, and at the day's close that pure gold light passes through us, heading for the other side. Even looking back, it is hard to get the measure of summer. It comes in all sorts of sizes: short and long, mid and high, and, following the latter, at Hawkwood there is Tall Summer, when the *Helianthus* in and around the Entrance Field and Old Kitchen Garden reach their British City Limits, as the gardeners' shadows ("the best fertiliser", according to one Chinese proverb) lengthen across the beds.

Stature is an important consideration in a garden, even, or perhaps especially, in productive ones. Trees, shrubs and hedges provide this for us, though mostly at the margins. Amongst the crops themselves, beyond the big top of trained climbers inside the hothouse, reaching for the sky has been a bit of a stretch for us. We've always grown (or rather tried, with varying but limited degrees of success, to grow) dwarf French beans outside: I consider the assembly and disassembly of all those strings and poles too much of a faff. Perhaps that's a bit rich coming from someone who insists that we make all our own seed and potting compost from scratch, but with food prices so low, growers should embrace richness wherever they find it.

For a while, sweetcorn were the jolly giants of the field veg, but they've been grounded after 2012's Squirrelgate fiasco. Since then we have turned to those that turn to the sun.

The Helianthus in question are H. annuus, the sunflower; and H. tuberosus, or Jerusalem artichoke. The former are dappled about the Asteraceae beds, and only now bursting into flower: rising suns as the one in the sky wanes. Children sometimes remind us that this is one of the most cheerful sights, period. I've been equally cheered this year by Jerusalem Drive, our new row of artichokes that lines the approach road to the Nursery's glasshouse and buildings, as if to a Promised Land.

They haven't put out their mini-sunflower blooms yet, and some years they never do. But they are taller even than their radiant ornamental cousins. A must for any ornamental vegetable garden, Jerusalems are a winter vegetable supreme, taken in moderation. Eaten to excess, or by the particularly prone, they inflict a flatulence verging on painful: you really can have too much of a good thing. People get wind of their windy reputation, so perhaps they will always be a delicious but marginal vegetable in polite society.

This probably explains the woeful lack of varietal choice. "Fuseau" is what everyone grows, as its tubers are large and smooth-skinned. But truth be told it's a bit watery and we grow the red-skinned "Gerard", whose stubby shape and firmer texture make them, I reckon, preferable but not more profitable. And they're your only readily available options.

The planning of Jerusalem Drive last winter presented an opportunity for exploring more obscure cultivars, something we generally have a good track record of. Helianthus tuberosus is native to North America, whose Native population cultivated it with gusto. You'll find a colourful array of diverse looking artichoke roots on US websites such as that of Seed Savers International, but getting hold of exciting propositions like "Passumpsic" – a strain reputedly cultivated by the Abenaki people before Columbus and his followers brought a virtual stop to indigenous plant developments – proved to be unfeasible.

And quite right too. The acquiring of heritage varieties with a rich precious story should perhaps be something governed by the wide web of human relationships, not by the ability to pay in plastic over the internet. Jen, our Employment & Enterprise Worker, gladly agreed to add "artichoke mule" to her list of responsibilities when travelling love miles to the States at Christmas, but returned similarly empty-handed.

But it can't end this way. Aimée, the Apprentice, had stopped off at Berlin's Tempelhof community gardens during the 2012 PEDAL tour, a cycle ride from London to Palestine, sharing seeds and solidarity all the way. The gardens are set on West Berlin's abandoned airport, and so have, at the very least, a symbolic vitality, as we try to combat climate change (towards which inappropriate air travel is a disproportionate contributor) through local food growing. She returned a year later, and recalls two Turkish, or perhaps Kurdish women, stuffing purple tubers into her hands. These were brought back and completely forgotten about, allowed to shrivel to within an inch of their lives until remembered like a distant dream and resuscitated in wet coir.

The Level 2 course planted out the four sunchoke "seed" in February at the very entrance of Jerusalem Drive, and now the mauve stems tower above the Gerards, and pretty much everything else, at 3.9 metres, or 15' 4" in old money. They're every bit the distinct, enchanting new variety we were craving. More than that: they seem, in all their glory, to be touched by some weird magic.

If there's a moral to this story, it's mainly this: a good artichoke is hard to find. And also that, sometimes, not always but often, if you fix the intention sure enough, the universe provides. Often, it's from another direction than the one you were looking in. The winter's evenings of wishing on a screen, and Jen's mission impossible, maybe helped bring into being our new sky-tickling artichoke variety, not from the Wild West, but much, much closer to home, via a compassionate Journey to the East. All along, what I was searching for was squirreled away at the bottom of Aimée's bag, and strangely enough, this is a simply beautiful thought.

October

The Day Dawns (2013)
The time has come to harvest the squash in the Old Kitchen Garden

Catching Some Sun

October 5, 2010

It's at precisely the point at which autumn's consolations of vivid colour begin to appear that I become prepared to accept that the game's up: the growing season is all but over, all but a dream.

Here at Hawkwood, the sumach and American hawthorn are the first to slip into the shades of sunset; the leaves of our subtropical guests – squashes, melons, basil – are shrinking to ashen without such joyful ceremony; my spirits could go either way.

It's a good time to be enjoying beetroot, I think. We're growing "Bull's Blood" and "Golden Detroit", both names accurately reflecting the hues of root and branch, and reflecting the proud tree leaves before The Fall. I'm pleased to say that the local appetite for this generally underrated vegetable has been such that we will have little or no need to elaborate on winter storage for them. However, no authentic seasonal food project is worth its salted cabbage without making some attempt to keep summer's abundance through the lean months of winter.

The leeks, kale and winter salads will stand out stoically in the ground. We'll squeeze the last drops of sunshine out to dry the chilli peppers and cure the squash skins, so that both can hibernate until awakened by the fire of the cooking pot. At the Hornbeam Café last week, my friend Ida was demonstrating traditional Italian methods of preservation – *passata* for tomatoes and *sott'olio* for vegetables such as French beans, courgettes, aubergines and mushrooms. At our Open Day last week Hornbeam chef Juannan led a team cutting a sizeable swathe through our basil jungle, making as much pesto as we had jam jars. Most have sold straight away, and to be honest I'm not sure how many jars will see in the winter, if the rate at which I have consumed mine is anything approaching average.

We are pasteurising fresh pressed apple juice; making cider vinegar; Marlene is no doubt racking up the chutneys as we speak; while my wine rack is brimming over with summer homebrew and my celery sauerkraut micro-project is surely heart-warmingly optimistic, if nothing else. Like nothing else, those jars and bottles of captured summer bring comfort as we head downhill, totems of a season not wasted but relished lingeringly. First, make things last.

Chilli Sufficiency

October 25, 2010

Contrary to what some people might expect, neither I, nor my illustrious colleagues at OrganicLea, have ever aspired to *self-sufficiency* as an objective or philosophy. Ecology, and any sort of humanity, is so much about beneficial relationships. Many would like to grow more of their own food, but if that is at the expense of sharing and exchanging food with others, then the net sum of experiences may be impoverished, rather than enriched.

Which is why I'm happy as a potato in mud to be a community market gardener: happier to grow ten kilos of salad and send it off to our box scheme, in order to get back one bag of salad and the chance to appreciate the wonderful organic carrots and onions grown by our compañeros in East Anglia, in the vegebox. It seems to me that it's neither consumerist dependency or self-sufficiency but *self-reliance,* that balance of autonomy and collectivity, that remains the hopeful path. And this does not deny the pleasure of sometimes *doing it all yourself.*

Early on in my horticultural journey, a member of the 1 in 12 Club's Peasants Collective in Bradford[55] explained away their disproportionate swathes of garlic as "something you can be self-sufficient in". This crop remains a good tip for any gardener who wants to experience the unique satisfaction of a year-round supply from their own patch of earth. Culinary herbs, such as sage and rosemary, need only a plant or two to fulfil that role. As we dug out the remaining potatoes from the field on Friday I reflected that our modest spud bed has comfortably yielded enough for the average annual requirements of three Brits, or ten people in China. (But only one month's supply for the average Irish peasant in the nineteenth century!)

If, as we do, you have a bit of protection, then for that hit of self-sufficiency, it's all about chillies. My favourite remains "Ring Of Fire", a cultivar that guarantees reliability without compromise – these are HOT chillies, as testified by the very sparingly excavated bowls of pepper paste left on the tables at our World Food Day Feast last week. These filled my doggy jar which, even accounting for the distinct possibility of a year of prodigious curry making, should keep me going until 2011's thin fruits are ripe for the picking.

Most of their brethren are on the glasshouse staging, drying sizzlingly, or still ripening on the plants. The plan is to string these fully dried peppers into "edible decorations", to add their joyful red glow and hearty warmth to the midwinter festivities of, hopefully, hundreds of average, and less average, British households. This, I think, will be sufficient.

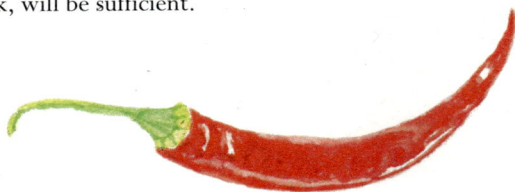

A Light Chilli

October 5, 2011

The season's gone out in a blaze of glory: thirty degrees of roasting October. Across the country, folk seized the summer swansong by the throat, getting out to light barbeques, jump into water, or just do a spot of beer gardening. Thankfully, the mutterings of a tiny minority of misery guts, moaning about their winter salads bolting prematurely, were not able to dampen the festivities.

I'm not proud to be that guy, though I'm now pleased to report that, while the heat has not been typically autumnal, the misty dews have, keeping the soil moisture levels up and helping to stem the feared splitting of leaves to the flowering side.

Plus, as any other New Town boy could tell you, it's all roundabouts. And swings. The tomatoes keep rolling out of the glasshouse like spilt drops of sun, and the Indian summer has coloured the cheeks of many of the pot-grown chillies. The latter are a sideline that have taken up far more of my attention this year than sidelines are really entitled to. But after the January trip to Mexico, I returned a *hot head*, determined to make Hawkwood a Centre of Chilli Excellence.

The Mexican "Jalapeno", the "Hungarian Hot Wax" and "Ring of Fire" (a feisty little number, weighing in at 80,000 "Scoville Heat Units" (SHUs)), are expected to do well, under protection, in Southern England, and so they have. This week they were abundant and red-ripe, as Jazz and I picked to fulfil the box scheme's annual spice allowance. But now, the more marginal cultivars are starting to ignite, like "Serrano", brought back from the highlands around Puebla, now close to cropping in our little London valley. At 8,000 SHUs, it's mild enough to have room to pack some flavour with its punch, and some Mexicans eat it raw as you or I would an apple.

Rising up the scale is Scotch Bonnet "Safi", and Shazida's Bengali variety, a birds eye type. They're ready to eat, but we haven't yet dared to. Only the "Chocolate Habanero" looks in danger of failing to provide any decent fruit whatsoever. Our headline act, "Bhut Jolokia", officially the world's hottest pepper at over one million SHUs (about half the strength of pepper spray), is rising by the day. Still green, but it's only a matter of time...

From being pots in the corner, dwarfed to insignificance by the summer beans and cucurbits, the glasshouse is now all about these bright little capsicums. There's something about sliding into the year's dusk with flames in our eyes and fires in our bellies. And, to misquote the Dalai Lama, if you think you're too small to make a difference, try eating a raw chilli. [56]

Lost and Found

October 16, 2011

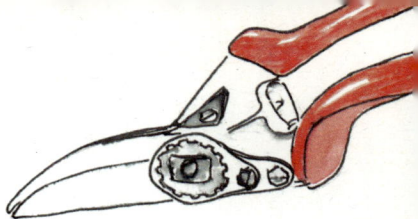

"Every time I see an adult on a bicycle, I no longer despair for the future of the human race."
- HG Wells

There is something uniquely wonderful about bicycles, and Hawkwood Community Nursery depends on them for transportation of many of its workers and produce. Yet I believe this sense of redemption expressed by HG can be experienced by gazing at any well-made, human-powered tool. Secateurs, for instance.

I pretty much always have a pair about my person when on site. To the casual observer, wearing a blade in a holster while performing admin tasks may seem like an affectation. But if I were to disarm, invariably I would soon find myself in the garden or glasshouse naked; in nature, there's always something in need of a passing prune.

I use Felco No. 8s. There's a pair I've had for eight years or so. They are mainly used for harvesting cut-and-come-again salads. Some folk use scissors for this task, but then you can't also use scissors for fruit tree pruning, clearing paths of bramble runners, severing cabbage heads, executing slugs, slicing cucumbers, opening parcels, cutting wire, scoring benchmarks, tightening jubilee clips, shortening irrigation pipe AND hammering in metal stakes. To be fair, you can't really use secateurs for the latter either, though a brave attempt to do so has lent my pair its distinctive appearance. Such scarring has, as in all human-tool romances, deepened our bond. The point comes when a piece of equipment feels akin to an extension, if not a part, of one's own body. Some might say that's a good point at which to try making do without.

This summer, I lost my Felcos. I've dropped them, and misplaced them, many times before, but this time they never came back when they were called. It may be foolish to grieve over inert material objects but, to lose something you are –literally – attached to, can only be a *loss*. And with it, I lost my sense of place in the garden. For, after my senses – almost equal to my hands – by-pass pruners are my main instrument of interaction.

I had to buy another pair of No. 8s. Brilliant, but they felt like an expensive, glitzy parody of the Old Faithfuls. Still, they cut lambs lettuce keen enough, and began to warm to my hand as the sun lowered into the October mist.

This Thursday in the Entrance Field, sowing field beans, performing a final weed and tidy, picking through the old squash bed. Their leaves, once so broad and green, now dry and shrivelled, shrunk to reveal three missed orange fruit, and the exposed red and silver – and new rusty mottling – of my original gardener's best friend, back from the dead.

Mourn not for the end of summer! Here, at least, it took a bit of death to retrieve something precious.

No Has-Bean

October 25, 2011

"An old man is setting a row of broad beans. So small a row, so shakily, dibbing a hole for each by jiggling a twig in the ground until it has made a space large enough. His allotment runs to the narrow verge between the cliff of chalk and the sunk road; right on the edge of an arm of the cove where the lorries enter. Balanced up there he sets his broad beans, while many shovels eat away at the ground below him. In three months they have taken this huge bite out of the hill: it will take three months from now for his beans just to be in bloom. Once he was a ploughman driving a team over a hill. Now, shakily on this little remnant of allotment, he sets a few beans. Because it is the time of year: it is time to sow beans."- Adrian Bell, Men Of The Fields, 1936[57]

I mean to enrich rather than make light of the above quotation when I say that, while the myriad of diverse gardening philosophies and techniques can appear bewildering, one basic line in the loam can be drawn. There are those that sow their broad beans before winter, and those that set them after it. My old man is of the latter school, whereas I have since gone over to the dark side.

This week, the focus of energy at Hawkwood makes one of those decisive seasonal shifts, from nurturing annual plants to maintaining and developing the woody plant stock and garden infrastructure. Good timing, if I say so myself, for a punctuation mark in the form of a week's leave. So I return to the family home, and a concerted attack on the ivy choking the old Prunus hedges. Somehow, though, I couldn't clock out without getting a first sowing of "Super Aquadulce" beans into the Old Kitchen Garden.

When I was growing up, I spent most of my time in the front garden, where ball sports were permitted. The back garden, in contrast, was put down to vegetables, fruit and herbs. Every main meal would have some homegrown component: perpetual spinach fresh from the ground, or summer fruits back from the freezer. There was no fanfare; this was *just something you did*. If you had a bit of ground, it was – and remains – simple common sense to utilise a portion of it for the kitchen.

Now us kids have flown, my mum continues to rise to the challenge of ensuring the bounty of plums, apples and goosegogs are picked, stewed, frozen and consumed just in time for the next annual round of picking. The old man, on the other hand, has in recent times made into a New Year's ritual the declaration, "well, I'm giving up on the garden this year". Each year, given his waning health, it seems a reasonable decision. Each year, as spring peers closer in, a packet of bean seed appears from nowhere on the sideboard; then you'll spot a few pots in a makeshift cold frame or a string line erected out the back, annotated with the label "B BEAN FEB". No fanfare, no U-Turn, it's just what you do.

What unites the two sides in the Great Bean Divide is that they both regard the sowing of these *Vicia faba* as a rite of passage. It's either the very end, or the very start, of the season. And either way, when it's time, it's time. Seize the day.

The Comforts of Celery

October 9, 2012

Saint Celery's is here! This esoteric festival, reported on these pages in May 2011, has arrived later than usual this year. In April, the first five pale leaflets – little hands of the Devil's Vegetable – groped out from the trays of Hawkwood's home recipe seed mix. Through the season, the leer of the celery beds grew greener and fuller across the Entrance Field, and now we cut them and tickle them around east London, arousing passion and suspicion wherever they go.

We left it late this year, hoping, after the slow start, for a last ditch stalk-swell. As is so often the case, what we've gained in size we've lost in good looks, as leaf spot, leaf miner and bare old age come to discolour the leaf. Yet the ribs stand firm. Unlike other plantings, we never worried for this bogside vegetable in the months of waterlogging. So much at home is it on our heavy drop of reclaimed marshland, it has attained a totemic status here at Hawkwood, where for a period a year – this one – it eclipses the basil as the overpowering Flavour of the Month.

Pariicuarly flavoursome in soups and stocks, I have been enjoying it in combination with potatoes this last fortnight. More poignantly perhaps, as this year the stores of humble spud will not outlast the stands of green celery as long as we are accustomed to.

Our first early spuds barely cropped, and our maincrop, the fantastically flavoured "Arran Victory", yielded a marketable, storable yield of a mere five kilos, after the slim pickings had slug and wireworm damaged tubers graded out into the "Team Veg" shelf for Hawkwood workers. In a good year we would have expected to bring in that amount hundredfold, enough to stock the farm stall into spring. We are not an isolated case. This year, the wet early summer has meant the majority of UK potato seed either weren't planted at all, rotted in the ground, were devoured by slugs, or suffered the blight. Our rural partners, Hughes Organics, are issuing dire warnings of potato shortages.

The supermarkets will, as ever, trample on whoever, wherever, to ensure continuity. For community food systems like ours, the lack of our perennially totemic staple will provide a sore test of creativity and resilience. Hannah, OrganicLea's new Produce Coordinator, is already facing up to this challenge, working out where we might stockpile, and where we can confidently endorse palatable substitutes – anything from pumpkins, to swede, to turnips, to parsnips, to artichokes, to oca, all depending on the recipe – for box scheme members' substitution.

Somehow we'll get by. Our greedy business leaders might leave us to rot, but they daren't let us starve: that's for export. Even in the darkest times, there will always be the next seasonal saviour to come through and enliven, enrich, nourish our meals: that, after all, is what vegetables *do*. There will be salsify, sprouts, beetroot, leeks, winter squashes in 57 varieties. Let us eat kale. And for now, praises be to St. Celery.

Pretty Deliciously Autumnal

October 16, 2012

When next you hear someone talk about the need to intensify food production to meet increasing requirements, bear in mind that all studies, experience and common sense have it that the most intensive mode of growing is the very small-scale: subsistence and peasant production. Community gardening, meanwhile, is highest in intensity of energy, information and relationships that are fed in and harvested.

For the community market gardener, this can be intensely challenging. For example, many a crop is lovingly raised and set out here in response to a request from the wider community, but life, especially in London, can speed faster than the seasons' pace. Chefs who have enthusiastically pledged to "take all the [basil/ celery/ Good King Henry/ salad leaves] you've got" when we are drawing up our planting plans, aren't always hanging around when we return triumphantly brandishing the green stuff. Granted, nine months might seem like a long time to process an order, but hey, we don't *make* the laws of nature.

Last week we finally rotavated in the bed of St. John's Wort that a herbalist had asked us to grow, shortly before they fled to the (admittedly herbier) pastures of the West Country. Gradually, sadly, you become more cautious towards such suggestions. But when Eleanor from Pretty Delicious (www.prettydelicious.org) showed up at the start of the year, she found a soft spot.

While at Growing Communities, I studied the work of Joy Larkcom, and decided that every bag of mixed salad leaves hence should, by rights, contain a free edible flower. At OrganicLea, we rigidly pursue this dogma, albeit sometimes stretching the definitions of "edible", "free", and, on occasion, "flower". The yellow buds of prickly gorse are harvested at quite a cost to the poor pickers, and don't taste that great, but tell me what other petals can you find in February? In the main season though, there's viola, nasturtium, shungiku, marigold and oyster plant, causing nothing but delight all round. I regard floral garnish as the signature of a really fresh, handmade salad, as well as adding a splash of vivid colour and their own unique nutritional and medicinal properties to the mix. In the garden, these flowers are vital for our pest management and also for our souls. As the Lawrence Strikers first put it, "give us bread, but give us roses".[58]

Eleanor has taken the edible flowers concept a step further, dealing in scrumptious bouquets. We've been stunned at the displays she's conjured up from our motley assortment of flowering herbs, bolting vegetables, companion plants and green manures. Each posy is sold with a card detailing imaginative recipes for the blossoms once they have cheered the dining table for a while.

As we approach our Produce Review and Planning Process for 02013, I'm looking forward to increasing and diversifying the floral tribute to Pretty Delicious. As autumn draws in, though, I've gleaned one further, unexpected yield from this connection. In midsummer, everything and everyone wants to flower. By late summer you have to look a bit harder. Last week, before Eleanor's Saturday stall at the Hornbeam Centre – flanking our veg stand – where had all the flowers gone? Garland chrysanthemum, mint, chive, borage, oregano: gone to seed heads every one.

Commencing picking veg with this in mind, my eyes were opened to the utter beauty and audacity of the late flowering – and fruiting – plants that are still out there: calendula, clover, alfalfa, ice plant, chamomile, hedge mustard, yarrow, shiso; rosehip, crab apple, hawthorn, blackberry, chilli: all ornamental and tasty. All to cherish, yet last year I barely gave them a second glance. Excitedly, I rushed to give Hannah regular updates on the latest botanical discoveries.

It's funny how things that start off sweet can quickly become nauseating. Double chocolate cake, say; or, I guess, scruffy men bursting into your office at random intervals and barking the common names of herbs at you. We soon agreed I should instead commit my findings to a written list. This I've done: our full mid-October menu of edible floristry products is simultaneously a chronicle that might prove half-decent reference material in years to come; and right now it makes for uplifting reading just as Jack Frost stalks the valley again.

"Have nothing in your house that you do not know to be useful or believe to be beautiful", said William Morris of Walthamstow, and I like to think he thought of the garden as part of the house. So should we all.

177

In the Pumpkin Hour

October 30, 2012

Last week you could hear the deer rutting in the twilight; in Friday's twilight, our piece of valley echoed to the hollow toll of the post driver, piling chestnut stakes through the vineyard. The Last Post rang out: then silence, as if sounding in the Pumpkin Hour.

For this week around Hallowe'en, the pumpkin attains the too-rare status of nationally celebrated vegetable icon. For true veg lovers, this is a double-edged carving knife: of those hundreds of thousands of Jack-O-Lanterns that will be chiselled out for Bewitching Night, most will pass to the other side without being first consumed by human beings. Those of us that do cook our grinning idols come All Saints will know that they may make good soupers, but have none of the versatility, flavour, texture or sweetness of a fine winter squash.

Our compromise position at Hawkwood is to grow "Uchiki Kuri", a good keeper with a rich honey taste and a dense, melting sweet potato texture; they are also big enough and orange enough to stand guard by the window without inviting ridicule from neighbours and zombies. That's what might happen if you employed our green-skinned, chestnut-nectared "Buttercup", or the "Sweet Dumpling", which look and cook up like a three-way cross between sweetcorn, round courgettes and, yes indeed, dumplings. Squash fans (let's call them "Squashers" to differentiate them from supporters of indoor racquet sports) will enjoy these Vit B-rich carb bombs for what they are, deep into the dark times, but they are decidedly not the heroes of the Pumpkin Hour.

The stipulation that vegetable lanterns must be watery, amber and as big as footballs is, though, a relatively recent transatlantic ruling. Originally, as reported in last week's Local Food News (OrganicLea's exclusive journal), the Celtic festival of Samhain, festival of remembrance, was marked by, amongst other peculiar practices, the turning of turnips and swedes into glowing skulls to denote the presence of ancestors. The tradition was taken to the Americas by Irish and Scottish migrants and refugees, and adapted to the indigenous Cucurbits which, let's face it, provide a bolder medium for scary sculpting. Then they came back to haunt us.

If it's hard to imagine a world in which swedes and turnips replace squash, try imagining a world in which they replace potatoes as the chief staple vegetable. Yet this world was Blighty before the "New World". Furthermore, turnip production was a staple job, as immortalised in the traditional Somerset folk song: "And zum delights in haymakin' and a vew be vond of mowin' / But of all the jobs that I like best, gi'e ae the turnit hoeing".[59]

So far from fashion has turnips' fall been, that they are now not far off being lumped with the (brilliant but misunderstood) likes of kohl rabi and Jerusalem artichokes in the "novel vegetable" ghetto.

At Hawkwood, we try to keep the turnip lamps burning, though the heavy clay is a mischief for root crops. In the last few days Jonny and Mary have returned from the glasshouse with a bounty of turnip tops. Latterly rebranded "Namenia" to suit modern sensibilities, turnip tops – leaves of *Brassica rapa subsp. rapa* – is what they are. In autumn and winter, they – alongside endive, chard, Bull's Blood, miners lettuce – provide that vital mildness to balance the rising hot and bitter flavours of our winter salad leaves. That mildness carries an unusual flavour that most people appreciate but find hard to describe: best described, I find, as, "turnipey".

The salad has slipped through the late summer gap, and we now have good dense stands, inside and out, red and green and going home, that should see us, and all of our kin, 'til Christmas.

So right now, we're all about salad and squash. Happy All Hallows: The Pumpkin Hour; Time of the Turnip.

Hunters and Gatherers

October 15, 2013

Our last Open Day was two weeks, but a whole season ago. On a still, warm day, Marko welcomed and pressed the gathering grapes as the audience pressed in; Vi worked wonders on the winter plant stall; while inside the building the "World of Chillies" workshop spun round again.

This year, it featured a live hot pepper sauce-making demonstration from condiment queen Mamma V; Hannah and Hannah took on the Pepper Medic role, circulating tasters followed by bread/ sugar/ milk pain relief; and three flavours of chilli vodka. The 2013 chilli collection was also deeper and broader, with eighteen cultivars spanning four different species and every continent on the planet, bar Antarctica.

Asia is headed up by the infamously ferocious "Naga"; Europe the sweet heat of "Romanian Yellow"; Sub Saharan Africa has "Bird's Eye", aka "African Devil"; Australasia, the great expanse of "Capsicum Joe's Long Cayenne"; and the Americas – the very birthplace and first stomping ground of the capsicum – give us "Bolivian Rainbow", "Ring Of Fire" (USA) and Mexico's searing "Habanero".

There are some shocking omissions: Southeast Asia, the Middle East, and China have no representation, despite chillies playing a zinging role in their respective cuisines. But I have confidence this will be remedied over time, with organic precision: for every (Caribbean) "Orange Scotch Bonnet" or "Hungarian Hot Wax" obtained from commercial seed companies, there is a "Rose" (Portugal) or "Little Girls' Fingers" (Brazil) that has been passed to us by hand: someone has, on their travels, found a particular pepper playing a pivotal role in the provincial gardening or cooking culture. They have then brought back the seeds, or fruit containing them, to Hawkwood, where we've grown them on, more than not with success, and true to type.

There are resonances here with the "Plant Hunters"[60], those celebrated botanists of the eighteenth and nineteenth centuries who travelled with early British expeditions to "uncontacted" countries. I hope there are some crucial differences too. Exciting as their adventures may have been, these men, such as Joseph Banks in Australasia and Robert Fortune in China, played key roles in the British Empire's exploitative mission. They plundered plants as an economic resource, using them to force open markets and destroy local economies with their export plantations. Everywhere they landed, they acted as if they owned the place, regardless of who was already there living on the land. Plants, men, and ultimately the land itself were taken without asking, and with violence if any objection was raised.

The narrow worldview that enabled such behaviour is epitomised by the fact that few plants from that era retain the roots of a local name; instead, they are christened with the self-important legends of that boys' club of botanists who happened to be strutting around the place at the time: so now we have Banksias, Bougainvillias, and Camelias in their dubious honour.

True, they were brave and excellent botanists, and merely men of their Age. Of course, that period of plant hunting and colonialism, married with our moderate island climate, gave us a rich diversity of garden and countryside that we now take for granted, which helped British gardens and gardening become truly great. It's hard to imagine Hawkwood, for example, without the liberation of spread and colour afforded by nasturtium and cucurbit.

But the subsequent implosion of the Empire has sounded that, although we may celebrate the ends, the means didn't have to be like that. In London today, the essences of the world's cooking and growing styles are shared in restaurants, neighbourhoods and allotments, with something approaching a mutual respect and equality. Our chilli collection begins with an interest in, and consideration for, the lands and cultures from which the little fruits burst forth. Albeit we are in a privileged position to be able to embark on travels and specimen collecting, I see it as a plant gathering from the grassroots rather than plant hunting from the turret: a better place, I reckon, for a garden to spring from.

Now, after the Spring, the Fall; of leaves, rain and Celsius. We look ahead to plant hunting of different sorts: burrowing through the soil for roots and tubers – potatoes, artichokes, oca, winter radish – where once great flags of foliage flew; the scouring of the borough for unpicked apples and pears for our Scrumping project, crescendoing in Walthamstow's Apple Day this Saturday gone; and later, after the Produce Review is through and the night is burying us, the search through the seed catalogues, for home favourites and unchartered territories.

A journey ahead; for now, time to stand firm and take in the autumn blaze: the brilliance of both chilli fruit and of broadleaved trees.

Of Mice and Then Some

October 29, 2013

"For nitrates are not the land...and...carbon is not the man...he is much, much more; and the land is much more than its analysis. The man who is more than his chemistry, walking on the earth, turning his ploughpoint for a stone, dropping his handles to slide over an outcropping, kneeling in the earth to eat his lunch; that man who is more than his elements knows the land that is more than its elements."- John Steinbeck, The Grapes of Wrath[61]

As Hawkwood reaches the end of its Local Food Fund Supporting Change Supporting Impact grant, we can rest assured that it's been a fairly high impact year. Our volunteering and training programmes go from strength to strength, supporting a close community of growers and grocers and seeding skilled-up community gardeners across the spires and shires and even over the high seas: we are playing a micro-role in a community food movement whose radical ideals are naturalising, and may soon become natural.

By contrast, in the garden here, the natural seems to have highest impact when it appears somehow manipulated; exotic; introduced. The plants that have most stood out this year have been the high-rise sunflowers; the range, volume and, it has to be conceded, size of our super squash crop; the sparkling frostedness of the ice lettuce; the Great Zing of the Green Zebra tomatoes; and, rivalling all of these, the cape gooseberries have captured, and held to ransom, the imaginations of most people who have glanced into the glasshouse this summer.

Even at plantlet stage their unfamiliar shapes were drawing many a curious squint. Now, while the rest of the vertical veg lose their leaves, they form a dense, green, three-metre high hedge that crowds out the glasshouse door and the propagation tables. Harvesting them has become a favoured pastime here: with their velvety foliage, going to pick them is venturing into a soft-play jungle to gather golden lamps.

Neither is the eating experience "normal": a laced parchment of the calyx (or "cape" as I like to call it, though the cape of its forename refers to the South African landmass where it first achieved commercial renown. My Zimbabwean grower friend Sara knows them simply as "gooseberries", resulting in a hilarious misunderstanding involving us and the hard hairy ones) is peeled back to the round sweetie, a sugary melon flavour with the crunch of a pear and the Vitamin C punch of an orange. Most commonly seen as a garnish on "posh" cakes or in petits fours, our box scheme members have been having them as a regular treat in the fruit bags since August.

Physalis peruviana syn. edulis, to give it the name that reduces the risk of confusion, is a nightshade, so takes up space that might otherwise be occupied by tomatoes in the crop rotation. There are question marks as to whether it makes total commercial sense to grow them in preference, but these are entirely unnecessary given the economic miracle of our heavy cropping heritage tomatoes: obviously it makes precious little, but the luxury and beauty of the community market garden is that it serves many senses. Our financial enterprise is part of many elements, a bigger picture wherein social impact is a legitimate currency.

Visitors and harvesters are not the only ones to have been enjoying these edible Chinese Lanterns lately. Our farm mice have been too and, right now, after some difficult times with rodents of varying sizes and cuteness credits, we have struck a temporary entente cordiale. For one thing, they are consuming the entire, mouse family-size, berries: a welcome divergence from that infuriating habit pests have of taking small nibbles out of everything. As a result they are barely making a dent in the crop, and there's plenty for all of us. Furthermore, the tomatoes and, most importantly, the early broad bean seed (something they destroyed in its entirety, inside and out, last year) have got away Scot free. A close inspection of one of their resting places, by the leaf mould sieve, reveals that they seem to be supplementing their fruitarian diet with little else but the kernels of calendula seeds. Happy days.

My worldview is not so utopian as to assume that we have reached a panacea in our relationship with the "wee sleekit cow'rin tim'rous beastie". But while many of our "best laid schemes…Gang aft agley[62]", it's also true that many a radical plan comes together. Through the storms, the broken branches, the flood years and the drought years[63]; the wrath; on the shores of Cape Gooseberry, mice and humans kneel on the earth.

November

The Entrance Field (2013)
Last hours of cultivation as autumn descends

Changing Clocks
and Calendars

November 3, 2010

In the ecocentric Celtic calendar, Hallowe'en marks the New Year. And I reckon that if, by some bureaucratic howler, gardeners were put in charge of redesigning the nation's wall-planners, you'd find many of them starting in November.

It's by this point that crops from the growing season past should have been lifted, and in many cases the crop rotation enters its next annual cycle. As the afternoons darken, the season can be reflected upon, analysed, and plans and projects for future growth drawn up.

Here at Hawkwood, it is reassuring that we seem to be in step with this rhythm. We've just had our project workers' annual evaluation, and Roger has been feeding this year's crop yields into a spreadsheet, so we now know *exactly* how much beet we've successionally cropped from the end of June from our 55-metre bed (the answer is, of course, 150.5 kilos).

These red roots – and the spuds – are out of the ground, and we are just pulling the last of the celery. Only those exceptional stalwarts, the leeks and winter brassicas, remain out-standing in the field. We have planted out all the winter salads. Despite their billing, they yield heaviest in April and May, although the light cuttings through the dormant season are most welcome. Last week we began to wrestle with the build-up of weeds in the Entrance Field, in preparation for the moving on of the rotation heralded by the imminent appearance of broad beans, garlic and green manures.

It's all over for the tomatoes, that vegetable totemic of summer and the Lea Valley. The bittersweet smell of Marlene's vats of bubbling green tomato chutney gusting out of the kitchen seemed almost as seasonal as the fungal incense of leaves burning gold to brown. Our toms carried the hopes of the whole season when they were sown amongst the frosts of early March. They have yielded well and might have gone through to midwinter, but the blight and rats both found their way to them, and there are times when you have to cut your losses and make a clean start. Now seems like a fine time.

The Coming Age
of the Fruit Trees

November 24, 2010

It was a glorious Kitchen Garden this high summer; but, standing in it trying to mark out garlic rows in the pressed clay, we see that the Entrance Field is once more just that: a field. And a muddy field at that: stand there for too long and I'd lose my wellies. What plants remain, whether here or under glass, have slowed to standstill: there is no more to be done. Now I have to confront the annual bout of existential puzzlement: what does it mean to be a Grower when it's not the growing season? Is it to be basically the less amusing equivalent of a pantomime horse outside the panto season? Do I exist? Is there really more to life than vegetables?

I was pleased to resolve the latter philosophical question at the weekend. The answer is of course: "yes, fruit". I re-learnt this at the "Fruit Growing Essentials" course we hosted at Hawkwood. Of course, fruit is no longer dripping from trees in gardens and waysides across the land. But in one of nature's many serendipities, down time in the vegetable gardening calendar corresponds to a spike in activity when it comes to tree and shrub care.

On the course we pruned apples, worcesterberries, blackcurrants; we dug planting pits for cherries. My thoughts began to turn to the cherry orchard, Entrance Field espaliers, Raspberry Row, and the late apple orchard we will be planting in the winter. These features could last a century or more, making them pretty important and worrisome projects in the planning: so as a collective we've delegated it to Sean to have most of the sleepless nights over them this year – albeit backed up by the considerable might of the Fruity Friday gang and their arsenal of slashers, spades and mattocks.

As tree-planting season arrives, these projects will come into sharp focus for us, so it's good to feel in a position to give them a bit more attention, and Sean a bit more support. Alas, a pantomime horse does not a cavalry make.

Picking Patient Peppers

November 9, 2011

The changes have been ringing around the glasshouse this last couple of weeks. The sheer green curtains of tomatoes and beans – seasonal furniture – have been drawn away, and we are reduced to the slight carpet of winter salads.

The tomatoes have been a particular triumph of interior design this year, situated as they have been in the north bed of the West Wing, peering in, directly and curiously, on the organised chaos that is the nursery office. So throughout the season, as the workers have gone about their admin, the cordons have crept up the view, ultimately filling it and pressing their red cheeks against the glass, like out-of-time Christmas trees with baubles across the room. The room that is barer now, no matter what screensaver we might load onto the computers.

From difficult beginnings, the "Kew Blue" climbing French beans (beans which, our Parisian volunteer Paco assures me, the French seldom eat) quickly screened off the potting benches from the rest of the glasshouse, had a fine year, and were received well wherever they went. As we unwound the crispening haulm from their string supports, we were able to retrieve enough ripe seed for planting next year; some for eating as a pulse – for ourselves if not the market; and a few for seed swaps, to get this rare and beautiful heritage cultivar disseminated wider.

The only survivors from the sub-tropics are the peppers, which just keep on, slowly but surely, until the hard frosts come. The sweet peppers have been in the wars: rats gorged themselves on them for a while, and blossom end rot has been an ongoing problem, in spite of redoubling our efforts to get the irrigation levels right. So yields have been low and some time ago I largely wrote them off, deciding to focus time and attention on more promising candidates.

Then last week, on the last note of the tomatoes' swan song, the peppers piped up with a good crateful of red fruit to brighten the farmers' market stall on a chilly Sunday in November.

Autumn, or rather, every season in the garden brings such reminders of how fundamental patience, alongside responsiveness, is in this game. And this was one of the subtexts of OrganicLea's tenth birthday party and awards ceremony last week. Introducing the awards, Clare likened the project's growth to that of an apple tree: we are now fruiting, but only after much patient plodding and formative pruning. It also *takes a long time to grow old friends*, as they say, and there were a heart-warming number of those in evidence on the night. At the Occupy London Stock Exchange on Tuesday night, Reverend Billy preached on the "radical patience" required to build *communities of resistance*.

Maybe time is on our side after all.

Field Day

November 21, 2011

At the "fag end of the year" (as one John Moore termed it[64]) comes the light at the end of a long journey in the Entrance Field. This was the week the sheet mulch finally reached the swale.

The Entrance Field looms kindly down on everyone who passes through the nursery gates. It's just shy of an acre, leans west-southwest, and is the fabled "open, sheltered site" of gardening textbook mythology. It's a far cry from the same literature's "fertile, free-draining, moisture-retentive soil" though. Nonetheless, it has been selected as our main area of *field vegetable* production, due largely to its proximity to the glasshouse and warehouse – the *centres of energy* – but with some consideration for the pleasing sensation an acre of mixed vegetables might create in people who two seconds ago were in London Town.

The standard method of converting pasture / meadow to annual plants would be to get in a man with heavy machinery to plough it up. But this takes its toll on soil structure, and we like to Do It Ourselves here. Instead, we opted for the permaculture method of *sheet mulching*. In this instance, this involves laying sheets of cardboard on top of the grass, laying a couple of inches of green waste compost over it; adding a layer of time – six to twelve months – then planting through the mulch into the dead and rotted lawn beneath.

Two other ingredients are essential: crazed cardboard collectors called Forest Recycling Project, and a small village worth of hands. It was one Open Day in summer 2009 when Growing Communities' grower Sara Davies and her visiting cousin Robyn began clearing the field, covering one small corner of a vast expanse. It took a good few trips back and forth from the far-flung compost pile to achieve this drop in the ocean; in the same time one man and his machine might have turned half the field under.

But gradually, each month in the quieter seasons has seen the dark band of soil improver bleed gently up the hill, ushering up more rife vegetables and green manures as each year heats up.

As well as associated techniques such as sheet mulching, permaculture has a set of principles, based on observation of natural systems. "Use small and slow solutions" is one; "Everything gardens" another. Over two years after Sara and Robyn's first small step for vegetable kind, Stefan and Jo stood at the top corner and rolled out the final strip of black carpet. The bit in between was done by dozens of people of all ages, nations, abilities, walks of life, boot sizes and wheelbarrow driving styles. Very few people have set foot in Hawkwood in the last three autumns and managed to leave without being pressed into peeling parcel tape from cardboard boxes, or schlepping a barrowful of green waste up a slippery slope. All to a soundtrack of birdsong, heavy breathing, and laughter.

The Entrance Field, its beautifully darkened skin streaked green with agricultural mustard and cavolo nero, now stands as a monument to People Power. Of all the powers that be, this one holds my hopes for the future.

Cold at Bay

November 30, 2011

Last year a sharp snap; this year an easy gentleness in November's setting. There will be no mad, doomed rush to hold back the tide of frost from sun-worshipping crops. The peppers have been permitted to fully ripen, and will this week join their squash, tomato and sweetcorn sisters in the compost heap of rest, after fruitful lives well spent.

The borderline "winter" salads – "Lattughino", escarole, parsley – have already given off enough leaf this clement autumn to justify their selection, whatever happens from now on in. The outdoor sowings of beans – field and broad; garlic; and agricultural mustard, have all been permitted to lift their heads above the parapet, a reflection of their roots' extension. This will allow them to protect soil structure and fertility from the coming cruel months.

Especially enlivening has been the rich river of glistening veg that has continued to flow from the Great Outdoors and settle in the packing station – the central reservoir between the classroom, kitchen, tool shed and office – before flowing out into the unnumbered kitchens beyond. Rainbow chard, perpetual spinach, Chioggia beetroot, kales black and curly, cabbage, Jerusalem artichoke – it has been a delight.

Urban market gardening is but one element of the "alternative food system", and the emphasis is naturally on "just in time" ultra-fresh produce. Consequently, the low season means lean pickings, and a welcome opportunity for rest, reflection and planning; the provision of winter supplies, from store or large field, has been the preserve of those hardened hands out in the sticks. But as I ponder the draft planting plans for 02012, I can see an emotional, as well as an economic, case for extending our cold menu range.

In doing so, we may rediscover again that there are degrees of hardiness. Last year the Red Russian kale froze to death at -10°; while Pentland Brigg, from the Scottich uplands, stood as unruffled as curly kale can.

After a quiet year, the mild damp has brought the slug multitudes out from all over the terrace. A few hard frosts should see to them, soon. But not yet. Not. Just. Yet.

Crop Revolutions

November 15, 2012

In Yorkshire – where my local food ideas were formatively pruned – the tradition is to plant garlic on Guy Fawkes. Burnt to death on countless occasions, Mr. Fawkes' standing has recently risen, phoenix-like, thanks to the success of *V For Vendetta*[65] and the Occupy Movement[66]. Even before this, there was always some sympathy in God's own county for a West Riding lad having a go at the centralised power of Westminster, and planting garlic seems a better act of remembrance than many others on offer.

I like this interweaving of the horticultural, festival and political calendar, and Guy remains my garlic guide. But here in the belly of the beast at Hawkwood, London, we're working 2,300 garlic plants into six different rotations: a tall, thin order even if we gardened through the flare-lit night. This year the aim was to get the garlic – and all the outdoor veg – in the ground by Zapatista Day, the birthday of the Zapatista Army of National Liberation (EZLN) (17 November). Formed in 1983 by a few disgruntled Mayan peasants – people like us, sort of – the EZLN launched their revolution in 1994 not with dynamite, but with cut-out wooden guns, balaclavas, corn, poetry and bravery. Since then, they have maintained control over their communities in Chiapas, Mexico, and influence far beyond: the Zapatistas remain a potent symbol of land-based people revolting against the cultural bankruptcy of capitalism. Beneath the drying maize plants I planted fava beans in their honour, in their hour.

Three beds each of broad beans, field beans and garlic planted, then off the field by Zapatista Day, with time to spare. Sure, there'll be weekly forays out to pick kale, cavolo nero, Brussels sprouts, radicchio. But largely, we stand back from it, let it rest.

It's been a tiring year for the Entrance Field: a silty clay, still fairly low in organic matter; when it's wet it stays wet wet way after the skies dry, making it difficult to work and prone to compaction. Even though we operate a bed system and use only light machinery if any, there are times this year we've trudged out, the plants ready but the ground not, knowing we risk setting back the soil's development in doing so.

Fortunately, the rotation will come to the rescue. On the field, we run a ten-course rotation, designed not only to optimise pest, disease, weed and fertility management, but also to improve soil structure. Key to this is the two-year green manure ley – the Sabbath, or winter of the rotation: time of rest. Active rest, mind: right now, still in vibrant leaf and flower, the clover and alfalfa are the liveliest of all the beds on the field.

We may be a while from the Gregorian calendar New Year, but Hallowe'en marks New Year in the Celtic calendar, and the autumn plantings usher in the next year of the annual rotation. And so the crop rotation becomes a kind of clock – a calendar – splayed on the land: as real for the grower, and more deeply felt, than any digital display.

I remember my woodland and green building friend, Adrian of Wholewoods, once expressing his frustration at not managing to find a settled home by saying, "I've only got a few coppice cycles left". Vegetable cultivation has blessedly quicker returns: every year, we sink garlic cloves and lift garlic bulbs, but the earth moves under our feet, and in the misty atmosphere of autumn you catch yourself thinking it'll be another ten years before we next plant garlic in this spot, all things being equal.

All things being equal. Rotations; small revolutions. Long-term thoughts like fireworks in long nights.

An Open Letter to The Co-operative

November 12, 2013

Thank you and cheerio, Co-operative Bank, and please wait for your receipt. In the last few weeks, as a result of its bad debts, branches are crashing down and it has literally become more the property of hedge funds than the venerable Co-operative Retail Trading Group. While its spokespeople sincerely assert that the commitment to ethical investment remains, I can't help thinking that without the backbone of a democratic structure, the culture of fairness and responsibility is somewhat weakened.[67]

This might seem like a straying from a gardening column (though good gardens should always lead you slightly astray) but my particular amble from global justice campaigning to urban market gardening pretty much starts with this very financial institution. As a student agitating for the boycott of Lloyds and Midlands (now HSBC) because of their reprehensible role in perpetuating the Third World Debt Crisis, I became only too aware of the need to offer people positive alternatives: to build as well as destroy or, in my now-found horticultural parlance, to plant as well as pull up. The Co-op was never a panacea: it was still a bank, after all; but it represented, in theory and practice, a genuinely different, yet widely accessible, way of doing money.

Scroll on a couple of decades and, on Thursday, I sat amongst a very different cooperative, that of OrganicLea Limited, for our Annual General Meeting. Accounts duly dispatched, we pored over Roger's annual Top Of The Crops charts, which rank the performance of all the Hawkwood crops in terms of their yields – kilograms, and pounds sterling, per square metre. Hannah, our Chair, invited me to comment on the findings.

Overwhelmed by the sheer detail of the charts in front of me, I enthusiastically announced that Basil had slam-dunked in at Number Two. On reflection, this probably wasn't the kind of stirring invective likely to steel the huddled co-operators into redoubling their efforts to confront, at the grass roots, the triple terrors of climate change, the destructive food system, and the widening gulf between the haves and have-nots. As ever, it was only on the way home that I thought of something to say that might help add up the figures for the coop, and the wider cooperative group of volunteers, customers, supporters, blog readers. It goes something like this:

2012/13 saw us producing and getting to market over ten thousand kilograms of fresh produce. On one hand, that's a lot of grub; on the other, it's a drop in the ocean of groceries shipped in and consumed in this borough. This is why the other OrganicLea activities – the outreach gardens, the distribution of organic veg from the wide fields of East Anglia, and the System Change work (that does the pulling up), are so vital: Hawkwood can provide a practical demonstration, an education, maybe even an inspiration, but real movement depends on our doing it together.

That tonnage generated £42,000 gross income. At the start of the Hawkwood Community Plant Nursery four years ago, our business plan projected £48,000: an ambitious target that we're within a respectable salad's toss of. More impressive though, is that we did it our way, as Ol' Blue Eyes would have sung if he'd been a member of a coop. By which I mean we haven't "gone commercial". Only two of the twelve acres are in intensive veg production: the rest belongs to extensive fruit and wildlife. We grow what must seem like a frightening amount of "unproductive" plants to anyone business-minded: thousands of green manures and companion flowers. But these are central to our soil and pest management plans, and these in turn have been key to our year-on-year increase in yields of those plants that do actually pay the rent.

We grow heritage cultivars that are not the highest yielding, but which carry a song that needs to be heard. We nurture a diversity of species too complex to be ruthlessly efficient, but through which we've created a fantastically elaborate salad mix (seventy-two varieties of leaf made it into the salad bags this year) and a whole World of Chillies. Thank you, everyone, for believing in this.

And who, the astute bank manager might ask, is this we? That's perhaps the most impressive and confounding bit. We are volunteers, trainees, course participants, coop workers. We come together for the fun of working with nature, and the serious matter of making a contribution to a better food system, a better world. Of the coop workers, Jonny, Mary, Jo, Vi, Adam and Clare have been there, week in week out, to steer this great tractor of people power over the ridges and furrows of the seasons, but each person in the whole coop has spun an integral thread in the web that's held it all together: from Marlene's website wizardry to Huf's wondrous watering system to Brian's flair for fundraising.

So, at the end of a long, hard, sweet growing season, there is a tale between the lines of the Top Of The Crops table, one that should give us all a warm glow of satisfaction as the temperatures, productivity and hedgehogs drop off. Going forward, is there anything this little coop can learn from the plight of the big Co-op Bank? One obvious thing is that we can and should be cheerful now, in the knowledge that it won't always be rosy – or indeed tomatoey – in the garden. And it is a monetarist myth that growth, however much and at whatever rate, is always good: the organic grower knows that lush, sappy growth, the kind that results from an excess of available nitrogen, is a pest and disease problem in the making. Balanced growth, that's the thing: and in the cool times, little or none is only natural.

And, in the week that we harvested the Cherokee Trail of Tears bean seed, and began pondering sunchokes, it may be worth quoting another, earlier, American – a gentleman named Black Elk: "Only when the last tree has died, and the last river been poisoned, and the last fish caught, will we realise we cannot eat money".

December

Winter Visitors

December 15, 2010

Not long ago, as winter was just beginning to grip, we were honoured to receive our first visit from Lizzie and Grahame Hughes, crucial pieces in the OrganicLea jigsaw. Intensively growing on one acre of East Anglia under glass, they were members and employees of Eostre Organics, an organic growers' cooperative.

For around a decade, Eostre appeared to embody what a genuinely alternative food system might just look like: a member-owned business, pooling produce – including that of sister European coops – for marketing direct via market stalls or through community-based enterprises in London, their most significant local market.

Eostre were there in 2006 to help us respond to local demand for a regular, reliable supply of honest good food by launching our weekly market stall. The stall goes from strength to strength, and while this and the box scheme have both done wonders when it comes to stimulating food production from within the little Edens of east London, the operations rest on the span and volume of produce from the broad lands beyond.

Like so many small fishes in the murky financial pond, Eostre went under in 2008; but out of the ashes rose Hughes Organics: Grahame and Lizzie working with a core of ex-Eostre growers, ensuring that those London communities continued to access decent organic veg. Despite hard times and disappointments, the Hughes stay true to the ideal of "calling into being" grassroots independents: small change rather than big chains. It is a pleasure to be part of a simple, mutually beneficial relationship that bridges the rural-urban chasm. And not just because it allowed me to hear Grahame's thoughts on watercress cultivation.

Another recent visitor, to everywhere on this island, has been Jack Frost, rendering much produce unharvestable for the last couple of weeks. Fortunately, some of Hughes' mates had the foresight to pull stuff out of the ground when it was soft and the veg hard, rather than vice versa, so our members still got great produce. With temperatures down to minus six here, some of the salads have had the limits of their hardiness sorely, sorely tested. But with the thaw this week the "Pentland Brig" kale looked as unbowed and finely textured as ever; as triumphant as I felt.

Through the freeze we continued to harvest salad, and especially rocket, from under the glass. The difference this bit of protection can make at this time of year is stark, and another reminder of what an incredible resource we have here at Hawkwood. With the ground fleeced in snow, there has been a lot of indoor work, moving staging around to expose more areas for tough concrete breaking, for the soft opening up to soil. Keep moving else you freeze hard.

VegeBoxing Day

December 20, 2010

VegeBoxing Day falls on the Wednesday before Christmas, when members of OrganicLea's vegebox scheme – and no doubt other box schemers across the land – receive a bumper midwinter edition. The idea is to: a) deck the reused carrier bags with high-value festive treats, and b) stocking-fill them with two weeks' worth of groceries, so that our farmers and packers can rest merry too. Hawkwood's contributions to the parcel this year are: chilli garlands, salad and potatoes.

We are very pleased with how the chilli decorations have turned out. Sarah's design balances the furious red of the "Ring Of Fire" peppers with the calming green of noble bay leaves, and they look right cosy hanging up in the kitchen or on the tree. William Morris, local lad and pioneer of the Arts & Crafts movement, famously declared: "have nothing in your house that you do not know to be useful, or believe to be beautiful", and I think he will be nodding his beard approvingly at the way these spicy mobiles marry beauty and utility.

We have been steadily munching away at the abundance of salad we inherited from the age of the sun. Some has been lost to the shockingly hard frosts, and what survives cannot be expected to re-grow in temperatures that can barely pick themselves up from ground zero. So those receiving our mixed salad leaves are getting a rare, and – for the moment at least – finite product. I have begun dancing for a mild spell in January so we can at least keep up our weekly salad commitment to Table 7 restaurant: it's in the lap of the gods now.

The potatoes are "Arran Victory", the oldest surviving cultivar of the great Isle of Arran stable, dating back to 1918. So far we've kept these lilac-skinned pearls in Chingford for the exclusive enjoyment of Hawkwood workers and farm stall customers. But, it being the season of giving, and this spud being "probably the best roasting potato ever" according to Tamar Organics, it's time we shared with the wider community. Its exceptionally high dry matter is one reason for its great roasting characteristics, also making it an acclaimed masher. However, its poor blight resistance means that it has become an example of "how potatoes used to taste", and for that reason we too will take a break from it next year. But I hope to be able to grow this gourmet tuber every now and then for as long as I live.

There is a minor Scottish theme emerging this winter, with the harvesting of the "Pentland Brig" kale in the Entrance Field last week. As the name suggests, this cultivar originates in the Pentland mountains near Edinburgh. When I'm working with it I can't help thinking of the "kale yards", the walled gardens tended by Scottish crofters where greens, and especially kale, were cultivated to provide a booster of essential trace elements to meals based on the field grown tatties and neeps. The Highland Clearances – a particularly fast and violent version of the Enclosures[68] – put paid to much of crofting culture and its kale yards. It is said, though, that on the Highland moors today you can still make out where the crofters' well-manured tattie and brassica patches were: the heather grows thickest there.

Equally, I am hoping our crops will grow thickest on the site of Hawkwood Manor's Victorian Kitchen Garden. We identified the area through historic maps and soil tests, and after much digging – even through the snow! – we have planted one hundred early rhubarb plants in the deep crisp and even. Already the crowns buds, in which February's "champagne" stalks are latent, are starting to green up in anticipation of spring. The real activity is below the surface, but visible swellings above the parapet are a vital symbol of hope in these times.

The Pondering Season

December 14, 2011

I have a tea tray at home, illustrated with all manner of garden paraphernalia. It bears the legend "A Gardener's Work Is Never At An End", repeated around the lip. Some have taken tea with me and flinched at this idea. But unlike "a woman's work is never done", that phrase that sums up the endless drudgery of the undervalued housewife, I think positive interpretations can be made.

For one, the tray depicts a room where gardening tools are displayed resplendent on walls, gardening books adorn the shelves, and the tables are brimming with flowers and vegetables. The message is that gardening isn't work that you drag yourself out to and then come home to recover from: it is something you bring back, to decorate, restore and feed the home and mind environment. Secondly, unlike so much contemporary work and thinking, gardening is essentially cyclical, rather than linear. The gardening day, week, season, year, life, contains cycles within cycles. Under every moon there is something needing sowing or planting, but the where and the when is constantly changing.

This is the time of year when I come closest to feeling that the work is *done*. Last week I congratulated Edith and Gertraud on completing the last planting of the year – the second spring garlic bed under glass. Yet, in my mind's eye, the spring garlic has greened and gone to climbing beans: that morning I had unveiled/ dished out the draft planting plans, after a six-week process of review, consultation and pondering, alone and with coop members and our catering partners.

Pondering is a vital part of the gardener's work. Often it is performed "on the job", though the importance of giving dedicated time to high intensity pondering should never be underestimated. And we are coming up to slap bang in the middle of the pondering season.

As the verb suggests, liquids can be well employed as pondering aids, notably seasonal fermentations of plant extracts. But they are not the only tools of the job. The gorgeous low light in the pondering season is highly conducive to inner reflection, as are the long nights, the humming fires.

I don't want to waste them: with the planting plans done, the seed catalogues will be mulled like wine, and Resolutions made to change the substrate recipe, tweak the apprenticeship programme. We will meet up in warmth to chew dreams and schemes for alternative local food systems, and relish the scarce bright hours in which we can get our ponderings out in the open, spade or secateurs in hand, never at an end.

Holes

December 4, 2012

It was *bound* to fall. The broadleaves' autumn display has been extra rich, and run for weeks, but just one big gust can be enough to bring the decoration down, just in time for December's artificial decorations to go up.

Lower key, as the leaves settle into the soil, is the release of the annual Hawkwood Plants & Produce Review. Uncelebrated, but not without highlights: for example, for the second year running, our heritage tomatoes are our most successful cash crop, pound-for-metre. Cash is dirty, and like soil, one of the vital oils that keep our crazy idealistic venture going: the others being people power and Fairtrade caffeine.

This week, the frost penetrating the glasshouse means the tomatoes' swansong, after almost six months of cropping. But salad, our staple, will carry on regardless. Constantly changing but always there, for stall customers, restaurants and box scheme members, our mixed salad leaves are the only rival to tomatoes in terms of their impact. Not that all the feedback has been glowing: most commonly, people express disquiet at the high proportion of herbal, hot or bitter flavours present. This is something we will try to address in our planning for next year, but as ever it's a fine balance: if we were to exclude all "strong" leaves it wouldn't be the same fragrant bag of tricks. The impossible dream remains the perfect blend that will just about please everyone: a lightly dressed nirvana where strong and mild flavours, soft and crunchy textures, are in total harmony to everyone's delight and satisfaction. An apparently utopian aim, yet according to Hannah, "we're getting there".

The perfect blend is as elusive as utopia, because of the surprising unfathomability of *people*. Take mustard, for example: we grow "Giant Red" and "Green In Snow", and they grow best through the winter. Mel, our herbalist in residence, notes that this season coincides with when we most need the warming effect of mustard. Given this, and the fact that Roast Beef & Mustard is one of Britain's few prized culinary gifts to the world, it's surprising how many folk round here aren't that keen on mustard in leaf form.

We're still picking some lovely mustard leaves; and lambs and miners lettuce, endive and salad rocket are especially vibrant now, abiding while there's change and decay in all we see. The once great – always great – tomato plants join the chillies on the compost heap, and attention shifts from growing plants to the dormant season's tasks: woody plants, repairing, and laying the land. Last week's task list had a strong wintry taste: path laying, bed filling, gravel shifting, single digging.

Basically, Simone and I observed, we spent a day either making holes, or filling them in. After all the rich complexities of nurturing vegetables, it's funny it takes a year to remember that there are few things in this earthly existence more satisfying than making holes, filling in holes being one of them.

Making holes and filling them in during dark recessions is, of course, the detractors' parody of Keynesian economics. But at the real risk of getting tangled up in allegory, and depending on where the holes are and what for, it's not a bad way to run a winter garden.

Whiter Shade of Kale

December 12, 2012

Last week I strode up the Entrance Field to Poets' Corner: the scene had changed utterly. The earth had grown a snow-crust, pinked by the low, red sun's minor rise in the south-east. London lay down, cold and desolated, its thin air sharp as a blade. As the herbaceous world and the animal kingdom shrink away, what's left is washed into stark relief: daily desire lines of rook and muntjac get a publishing deal in pages of snow; Yates' Meadow, the green hill far away that spends its whole time peeping over at our naked veg, is finally exposed by the raising of the hornbeam curtain; the evergreen kales and Brussels stay static under fine-woven crop covers, yet loom more than ever.

The kales are at their best now. The freeze has put a freeze on slug attack, brought some sugars out to balance the bitterness, and as we pick our way up the stem, the leaves get ever young and tender, with reduced stalk and, in the case of Pentland Brig, more frills. Yesterday Adam and I picked it, frost-decorated: a picture greetings card from the distant North.

For over two thousand years, kale has been cultivated to be picked in weather like this, and much more brutal. Its extreme hardiness made it the winter green choice of, amongst others, the Scottish crofters, who spent their winters *kale yards* from sickness. The kale yards were areas close to the homestead, where dry stone walls sheltered the leaves from the arctic winds just enough to provide for humans and their sheep and cattle: an early example of "protected cropping" on these isles.

By the time protected cropping reached its zenith in the high-tech "Sea of Glass" across our Lea Valley, the low-tech crofters had been all but wiped out. First, they brought in the Enclosures, steadily driving the English peasant from the land; then, they came for the crofters, in a much quicker, more violent chain of events called the Highland Clearances, in the 18th/ 19th centuries. Now, but traces of the kale yards and tatty fields can be made out in the eerie quiet of the glens, where the heather grows thickest.

No final defeats. A few crofters managed to hang on to their patch of ground; still more retained some of their culture and history. And "what they could not kill, went on to organise"[69]: at the end of the 20th century, crofters and their allies began taking on the power of the lairds, winning back land and rights for their communities, eventually forcing land reform legislation through the new Scottish Parliament.

The Scottish Crofting Federation is a bit of a beacon, then, for communities taking back control of their food system and its mode of production – the earth. They are the only UK Members of Via Campesina, the global organisation of peasants and small farmers.

Whisper it in the wind: the crofters may soon be joined in Via Campesina by another UK group: an alliance of human-scale producers currently plotting behind garden sheds. If Via Campesina UK needs an emblem, they could do worse than the fluttering leaf of a certain winter brassica. When the going gets tough…

Brussels Policy

December 20, 2012

This year, the Hawkwood midwinter feast featured not Hawkwood potatoes, after this year's spud failure, but our very own Brussels sprouts. The bed of Brussels has been rising pine-like under the mesh on the Entrance Field since early this year mainly for this moment, at the request of Sophie, our then Volunteer Coordinator. Briefly stocking the stall and box scheme has been a merry spin-off. At the outset, I warned her that picking frozen sprouts with freezing hands is one of the most feared tasks in market gardening. The cold snap has turned mild though, and the snap of the buttons being plucked off the stalks is strangely, deeply, satisfying: like the pop of a cork out of a bottle. Jo rustled them into "Sprout Surprise", and with them fed the fifty, alongside roasted roots, braised red cabbage, nut roast, and onion gravy.

Christmas, Yule, Winter Solstice, Midwinter, Crimble, Xmas: call it what you must, think of it what you will: at the very least, it is a time when the population receive tidings of seasonal produce. Not always received graciously, it must be said: the Bird, parsnips, even mince pies, are eagerly anticipated then rapidly despised. But the greatest ambivalence seems to be reserved for "Britain's most hated vegetable": the Brussels sprout.

It is regarded as an essential part of the midwinter feast, yet denigrated as much as the cracker jokes. There are those of us that love sprouts, and those that regard them as horribly windy, soggy, bitter: sprouts divide the nation like Marmite, and the issue of Europe. I even speculate as to whether, in some folks' minds, there is a link between Brussels the EU HQ, and its eponymous mini cabbage…

The history of the Brussels sprout is reassuringly uncertain, but it does seem certain they arose in Belgium – where the earliest records of cultivation exist – though good cultivars have since been developed in Britain. Of course, most of the fayre swerved up at the traditional British Christmas roast will not, ultimately, have originated on this isle: even the stalwart potato, parsnip, swede are, at root, introductions. This has to be cause for celebration: we are a mongrel race, the weird result of wave follows wave of immigrants; refugees; invaders; captures; mixers; adaptors: in plants, as in people.

May your Christmas plates be steeped in tradition and diversity, and may they embody the give and take of rich cultural cross-pollination. At its best, that's what this festival, this country, this *Europe* is: a place of sharing; a displacing of austerity.

Happy Solstice. And may all your vegetables be cooked right.

Red as Any Blood

December 18, 2013

As autumn falls to winter, the quality of the rich, low light and fiery tree leaves is utter consolation. In the veg garden, it is the "radicchio" types of chicory that do this job, and sometimes more. For, with every drop of temperature the foliage ignites further from anonymous green to striking scarlet, crimson, pinks and whites. They liven up the tramp around what is now a drab muddy field; and also the salad mix. In doing the latter, they are in some way appreciated, for their visual contribution at least. The cold, as with parsnips and Brussels sprouts, also brings out the sugars. Most people still find them bitter though, and we have to be careful to keep the relative proportion of chicory to other leaves at no more than 20 per cent. Given the number of chicory sceptics out there, someone with an eye for customer relations might advise growing even less, in answer to which I would point out their stunning shades, and the fact they stand really well in autumn and winter. But the truth of the matter is that we grow an awful lot of chicory here for no better reason than Jo and I bloody love it.

My better half alleges that my championing of *Cichorium intybus* stems from the same basic psychological disorder that lies behind my fanaticism for ferrets and Stevenage FC: The Love of Unpopular Causes. This may work fine as an overarching theory – indeed I've asked for thirty-eight similar symptoms to be examined in this light – yet it neglects the complex set of interactions with the plant, that have led me to this place.

My earliest encounter was as a young boy: between the *Johnnie Walker* and the *Beefeater* on the kitchen sideboard stood a tin purporting to contain a bottle of *CAMP Coffee*. It was eye-catching, with its iconic image of a Highland soldier in full battle dress; in the background an Indian soldier and military canvas; and the immortal slogan "Ready Aye Ready".

For most of its life the CAMP tin contained not the eponymous product, but digestive biscuits: its presence there was one of nostalgic symbolism. For my old man, it was an everyday reminder of the war years: the mobilisation to fight fascism; the postwar socialist project; and the comforts of shared hardships, wherein rations saw that CAMP replaced "real" coffee. The beverage uses chicory roots in place of beans.

Years later, after a particularly heavy night of *discussion and debate* at the European Social Forum, I found what I now believe to be a bunch of "Catalogna Frastagliata" on a Paris market stall. I bought the dandelionesque leaves out of curiosity; then ate them like it quenched a thirst. My battered liver craved the restorative greens. These events set the stage for the emergence of chicory as Winter's Great Redeemer once I became a salad grower.

Redemption, that is, if you can keep it from rotting. Hailing from Veneto, Italy's coldest region, cultivars like "Rossa di Treviso" and "Grumolo Rossa" relish a cold snap: it's the dampness of our British winter – and our London clay – that they can't stand. It's fine on the terrace where we do successional cropping so the heads never get dense, but in the Entrance Field harvesting and cutting out soft rots is a combined mission, and by Christmas they're all over bar the carolling, pink palms, just a beautiful memory.

Not this year though: *not this year*. Cultural methods, cultivar choice and drier weather have combined to ensure we still have a fine red stand going into the festive salad bags and out the other end. This is in no small part due to Aimée, whose early attentiveness to disease kept it in check, in the same way that Gary swashbucklingly fought off both red spider mite and tomato blight in the glasshouse. Not that Aimee volunteered for these duties, but when she muttered, "I don't understand this chicory stuff" in summer, her fate was sealed: three months in chicory re-education camp. I like to think that, deep down, she's grateful for it.

Deep down into the longest night we go again. At the midwinter social there were ends: goodbyes to the trainees, and a fond farewell to Mary the Fruit Worker. Things look bleak. The radicchio torches, in the bags and on the land, hold the fiery promise of a brighter tomorrow. Redemption? Ready Aye Ready.

Endnotes

1. From Wendell Berry, *What Are People For? Essays*. Berkeley: Counterpoint, 2010.

2. Emma Goldman (1869–1940), anarchist, feminist, writer, orator and campaigner, actually said, "If I can't dance I don't want to be part of your revolution".

3. Oxford Real Farming Conference: www.oxfordrealfarmingconference.org established in 2010 as a parallel alternative to the corporate-sponsored Oxford Farming Conference.

4. From "Letter To A Young Activist During Troubled Times": http://mavenproductions.com/index.php/services/dr-clarissa-pinkola-estes/dr-clarissa-pinkola-estes-letter-to-a-young-activist-during-trou/

5. From the self-published poetry book *The New Black*.

6. "Let A Hundred Flowers Bloom" was a slogan of the Chinese Communist Party in 1957, meant to encourage free expression – or perhaps flush out dissenters – shortly before the start of the "Great Leap Forward" (1958). This is not really the space to debate the successes and failures of Maoism in practice, but, at the risk of being flippant, they had a nice turn of phrase.

7. Wholewoods Environmental Arts: www.wholewoods.co.uk.

8. St. Pauli was the name by which Growing Communities' first Patchwork Farm "micro-site" was known to myself and its first gardeners, Sean and Annie. Located in the grounds of St. Paul's Church on the Kingsland High Road, Stoke Newington, the added vowel served to salute St. Pauli Football Club, the Hamburg team renowned for their anti-fascist and left-wing supporter base. The name has never quite achieved official recognition. See www.growingcommunities.org/food-growing/patchwork-farm/ for more on the Patchwork Farm; http://en.wikipedia.org/wiki/FC_St._Pauli for a decent account of the St. Pauli phenomenon.

9. Red Hook Community Farm: www.added-value.org; Brooklyn Grange Farm brooklyngrangefarm.com; New York Greenmarkets: www.grownyc.org/greenmarket.

10. From the album *Overnight* (1998).

11. *The Land* magazine: an occasional magazine covering issues relating to land rights, rural life, agriculture, sustainable development and land access. See www.thelandmagazine.org.uk.

12. During the winter of 2013–14, the British Isles were in the direct path of several winter storms, which culminated in serious coastal damage and widespread persistent flooding. Record breaking winter rainfall led to persistent flooding on the Somerset Levels, with recurrent flooding hitting Southern England in the Thames Valley, Kent, Sussex, Dorset, Hampshire and along the River Severn. There were deaths, and thousands of homes and lives ruined.

13. Heritage Seed Library, a vital institution in the preservation of a living library of endangered vegetable varieties. See www.gardenorganic.org.uk/hsl.

14. Buenaventura Durruti (1896–1936), symbolic anarchist figure in the organisation of the anti-fascist militia during the Spanish Civil War 1936–39. The full quote is "We are not in the least afraid of ruins. We are going to inherit the earth, there is not the slightest doubt about that. The bourgeoisie might blast and ruin its own world before it leaves the stage of history. We carry a new world, here, in our hearts. That world is growing this minute."

15. Masanabu Fukuoka, renowned Japanese "natural farmer", whose books on the subject include *One Straw Revolution* and *The Natural Way of Farming*.

16. Paul Scholes, Manchester United and England footballer of the 1990s/2000s, a fine playmaking midfielder with a tendency for occasional wild, dangerous tackles that made him see

Onwards and Outwards (2012)

Visitors reach the West Bank Salad Terrace, the last stage of the July Open Day Site Tour cards as red as his hair.

17.   Joni Mitchell, "Big Yellow Taxi", 1970.

18.   Scarlet Heights is a hillside village in West Yorkshire, now part of the Bradford conurbation.

19.   In the 2013 "Horsemeat scandal", it emerged that foods advertised as containing beef, sold through major UK supermarkets, notably Tesco, were found to contain undeclared or improperly declared horse meat – as much as 100 per cent of the meat content in some cases – and other undeclared meats, such as pork. While not necessarily a direct food safety issue, the scandal revealed a major breakdown in the traceability of the food supply chain, and with it the potential for any amount of unsafe or taboo meat to end up on supermarket shelves.

20.   Iain Tolhurst of Tolhurst Organics, an inspirational organic market garden: www.tolhurstorganic.co.uk.

21.   Cropshare is a scheme launched by OrganicLea in 1998, aiming to stimulate the local food economy by enabling local gardeners and allotment holders to legally sell their sustainably grown, surplus fruit and vegetables through our box scheme and market stall. See www.organiclea.org.uk/ we-sell-food/cropshare.

22.   Margaret Thatcher, British Prime Minister 1979–90 famously claimed, "there's no such thing as society".

23.   Margaret Thatcher died 8 April 2013. During her leadership, the Tory government abolished the Greater London Council in 1985 as people kept voting in a left-wing Labour administration under Ken Livingstone. Amongst a raft of measures intended to improve life in London for all, the GLC financially supported the creation of ponds, as a lifeline to wildlife. "Tramp The Dirt Down" is a song by Elvis Costello in 1989, in which he looks forward to Thatcher's death: "When England was the whore of the world/ Margaret was her madam/ Because there's one thing I know, I'd like to live/ Long enough to savour/ That's when they finally put you in the ground/ I'll stand on your grave and tramp the dirt down." The final line was controversially tweeted by George Galloway MP in the hours after her death. To the disappointment of many who may have liked to act out the song, Maggie was cremated! "Thatcher's End" at Hawkwood was inspired by a coppice of the same name at Ragman's Lane Farm in Gloucestershire, which was planted on the day Thatcher resigned, in the face of widespread revolt against the Poll Tax, in 1989/90.

24.   Peter Kropotkin (1842–1921): scientist, philosopher, activist.

25.   The Regulations on the Marketing of Plant Reproductive Material Legislation were drafted by the European Commission in 2012. It sought greater controls over which plant varieties could be sold – as seed, seedlings, cuttings, plants. A vigorous campaign against it, headed up in the UK by Garden Organic and Real Seeds, saw the proposals rejected by the EU Parliament Agriculture and Environment Committees in early 2014; however it revealed the intention of the biotech industry to use the EU to pursue its aims of tightening its grip on the horticulture market, at the expense of biodiversity and small-scale growers and breeders.

26.   Whilst in organic horticulture it is generally held that tilling – inverting the soil through ploughing, digging or other similar methods – is detrimental to soil life, releases carbon in to the atmosphere and, in the long run, damages soil structure, there is a divergence of views over what constitutes "excessive". "No Dig" gardeners eschew any form of tilling, whilst many, including OrganicLea, see it as having potential advantages over No Dig in specific circumstances, e.g. growing potatoes, and the inclusion of green manures in a rotation.

27.   Sara Maitland, *Gossip From the Forest: The Tangled Roots of Our Forests and Fairy Tales*. London: Granta, 2012.

28.   Landworkers' Alliance: see www.landworkersalliance.org.uk.

29.   "Never doubt that a small group of thoughtful citizens can change the world. Indeed, it is the only thing that ever has" – Margaret Mead.

30.   *The Love of Worker Bees* (1923), a semi-autobiographical novel by Alexandrei Kollontai,

portraying the life of a woman in the immediate aftermath of the Russian Revolution, 1917.

31.   In the song "Ilkley Moor Bah'tat", the protagonist goes out courting without a hat, and the orator forecasts that he will, as a result, catch a cold, die, be eaten by worms and ultimately therefore, by his own people.

32.   The full and complete lyrics to this song run, "Celery, celery/ if she don't cum/ I'll tickle her bum/ with a lump of celery".

33.   For the latest in opposition to the growing of GM plants in the UK see www.gmfreeze.org.

34.   From *My Roots: A Decade In the Garden*. London: Hodder, 2006.

35.   BSBI = Botanical Society of Britain & Ireland. See www.bsbi.org.uk.

36.   Satori: Zen Buddist term for "the state of sudden indescribable intuitive enlightenment" (Collins English Dictionary).

37.   Growing Communities: community-led box scheme, farmers' market, urban market gardens and more, in Hackney. See www.growingcommunities.org.

38.   The Battle of Orgreave, 18 June 1984. Orgreave was a British Steel coking plant in South Yorkshire, where, during the Great Miners Strike 1984–85, mass pickets were organised to attempt to stop coal entering the plant. On the day of the battle, some 5–8,000 police officers confronted roughly the same number of pickets. It was a bloody battle; official figures state that 93 arrests were made, with 51 pickets and 72 policemen injured. In 1987 South Yorkshire Police paid over half a million pounds in compensation in an out-of-court settlement to 39 pickets, and the Orgreave Truth & Justice campaign – www.otjc.org.uk – continues to push for a full public inquiry into the actions of the police on that day.

39.   A landrace is a local ecotype of a domesticated animal or plant breed that has been improved by traditional agricultural methods and adaptation to its natural and cultural environment. The UN Food & Agriculture Oranisation (FAO) defines a landrace or landrace breed as "a breed that has largely developed through adaptation to the natural environment and traditional production system in which it has been raised." See http://en.wikipedia.org/wiki/Landrace, accessed 17 August 2014).

40.   In the UK elections to European Parliament 25 May 2014, the anti-immigration and anti-federalist UK Independence Party received the most votes of any party: 27.5%. Turnout was 34.17%.

41.   Dial House, an ex-farmhouse in North Weald, Essex, has been an "open house" since 1967, and host to an array of political, cultural, artistic and horticultural projects, amongst them the anarcho-pacifist punk band Crass (1977–1984).

42.   Matthew 7:16.

43.   Corinthians 11:24.

44.   One element of organic inspection and certification is that anything and everything applied to the soil and plants has to be declared and accounted for. If it is "brought in" from beyond the holding (growing site) it must have the prior approval of the certifying body: for example, dried seaweed meal. This is only right and proper, though it does pose an additional administrative burden on organic growers and farmers – which provides many of us with a good excuse for a grumble now and then. The real answer, of course, lies in reducing our reliance on brought-in inputs, which is kind of half the point.

45.   For an explanation of the five digit date, see viii in the Introduction Endnotes.

46.   John Clare, "Sighing For Retirement".

47.   Sustain, the alliance for better food and farming: www.sustainweb.org.

48.   Throughout August 2011, uprisings spread across London and throughout the country, sparked by the police shooting of Mark Duggan in Tottenham on 4 August. These had the general character of mass rioting – confrontations with police, looting and general destruction of property; however in many areas, attacks were focused on specific targets: institutions closely associated with the social

and economic marginalisation of young people. In Walthamstow, for example, this meant the banks and the Job Centre.

49.   Christiania is a self-declared autonomous neighbourhood of some 1000 residents in Copenhagen, Denmark.

50.   For more on food growing in Detroit, see the film *Grown in Detroit* (Mascha & Manfred Poppenk, 2009).

51.   As OrganicLea is entering the fifth year of its lease on Hawkwood Plant Nursery, Grow Heathrow celebrate five years of squatting land on the site of the proposed third runway. See www.transitionheathrow.com/grow-heathrow/.

52.   According to the United Nations Environment Programme (UNEP, 2011, *Towards a Green Economy: Pathways to Sustainable Development and Poverty Eradication* — www.unep.org/greeneconomy) small-scale producers are responsible for providing 70 per cent of the world's food. UK Food Group is the UK network for NGOs working on global food and agriculture issues. See www.ukfg.org.uk.

53.   Seamus Heaney, poet, born 1939, died 30 August 2013.

54.   PANSiEs: Politically Active Not Seeking Employment: a classification believed to be used by Department of Social Security in the 1990s/2000s.

55.   The 1 in 12 Club arose from Bradford Claimants' Union in 1981, and obtained a building in central Bradford in 1988, which to this day houses an anarchist social club, bar and music venue. See www.1in12.com.

56.   The Dalai Lama's actual quote is, "if you think you are too small to make a difference, try sleeping with a mosquito".

57.   Adrian Bell, *Men And The Fields*, Dorset: Little Toller Books, 2007.

58.   Lawrence Strikers: the 1912 strike in Lawrence, Massachusetts, successfully won improved pay and conditions for thousands of female textile workers. The slogan "We want bread, but roses too!" that emerged from it gave the strike the alternative name "The Bread and Roses Strike". "Bread and Roses" was taken up as a slogan, especially amongst the Wobblies (members of Industrial Workers of the World, the anarcho-syndicalist union — www.iww.org.uk) signifying workers' needs/demands for cultural and social gains, as well as economic ones.

59.   The Turnip Hoer's Song, also known as "The Fly Be On The Turnip"; a traditional song from Somerset & Wiltshire.

60.   For a good analysis of the plant hunters' role in the colonial mission, see Martin Hoyles, *The Story of Gardening*, MacMillan, 1991.

61.   John Steinbeck, *The Grapes of Wrath*. First published in the USA by The Viking Press Inc. 1939. Great Britain: Penguin Classics, 2000.

62.   From the Robbie Burns poem "To A Mouse".

63.   John Steinbeck's novel *Of Mice And Men* took as its title a line from the above poem. The final sentence of this entry references another of his books, *The Grapes of Wrath* (1939). The full passage reads: "The anger of a moment, the thousand pictures, that's us. This land, this red land, is us; and the flood years and the dust years and the drought years are us. We can't start again. The bitterness we sold to the junk man - he got it all right, but we have it still. And when the owner men told us to go, that's us; and when the tractor hit the house, that's us until we're dead. To California or any place — every one a drum major leading a parade of hurts, marching with our bitterness. And some day — the armies of bitterness will all be going the same way. And they'll all walk together."

64.   John Moore, *Come Rain, Come Shine*. Sutton, 1956.

65.   *V For Vendetta*, a graphic novel by Alan Moore & David Lloyd (1982), on which the 2006 film of the same name, by McTeigue & Wachowskis, was based.

66.   The Occupy Movement was inspired by uprisings in the Middle East, and swept through much of the world in 2011/13, with over 1000 occupations in 82 countries. It protested growing

social and economic inequality by occupying and setting up protest camps on or near land owned by public and financial institutions. The Occupy movement continues, especially through the 15M movement in Spain, and in the UK, for example through the journal The Occupied Times (see http://theoccupiedtimes.org).

67. In October 2013, the Co-operative Group, in the face of multi-million pound losses for the Group, and the Co-operative Bank in particular, agreed to sell off 70 per cent of the bank to US hedge funds Aurelius and Silverpoint.

68. John Prebble's *The Highland Clearances* (Penguin, 1963) provides a detailed account.

69. From the song "Joe Hill" by Alfred Hayes (1938).